T0147710

Critical Acclaim for Death Walkers

David Kowalewski writes in a clear and compassionate way, showing how sometimes, at death, it is necessary to perform healing work on a soul to help it transcend. This is an important book for the times we live in, for as people die more consciously, the more conscious the earth becomes.
   --SANDRA INGERMAN, MA, author of *Soul Retrieval*

Death Walkers deepens our imaginings about death, the dead, and our possible conversations with those who have departed from our everyday world. Drawing on first-hand accounts and cross-cultural research, David Kowalewski offers us an engaging Western perspective on the art and methods of the psychopomp. Anyone who's going to die will benefit from this highly readable book.
   --BILL PLOTKIN, PhD, author of *Soulcraft*

This is the most in-depth treatment of the subject that I have ever read. Using personal experiences to illustrate specific aspects of psychopomp behavior and activity is not only interesting, but very helpful to those learning about it. I also appreciated the chapter endnotes and the extensive list of references. Good job!
   --SERGE KAHILI KING, PhD, author of *Urban Shaman*

David Kowalewski has written a comprehensive book on one of the basic tasks of the shaman: psychopomp work. This is a highly readable, well-researched book, detailing a number of Dr Kowalewski's personal experiences as a conductor of the spirits of the dead. He makes a strong case for the need of more psychopomps in the modern world. This book is highly recommended.
   --DANA ROBINSON, co-author of *Shamanism and the Spirit Mate*

This important book is an informative ... thorough, cross-cultural overview ... Dr. Kowalewski speaks with authority ... as ... an experienced psychopomp and ... a near-death experience[r] ... and practicing psychopomp ... The text is further enriched with fascinating examples ... [and] conclude[s] strongly with a most important chapter on what these practices mean for our everyday living ... A very welcome addition to the literature.
   --PENNY SARTORI, PhD, author of *The Wisdom of Near-Death Experiences*

Listen to Dr. Kowalewski describe his psychopomp work during an interview with Christina Pratt, author of *The Encyclopedia of Shamanism*, on her podcast program, *Why Shamanism Now* at http://whyshamanismnow.com/2015/07/psychopomp-to-conduct-the-souls-of-the-dead-with-david-kowalewski/

ALSO BY DAVID KOWALEWSKI:

Deep Power: The Political Ecology of Wilderness and Civilization (Nova Science)

Dynamic Models of Conflict and Pacification: Dissenters, Officials, and Peacemakers (Praeger)

Global Establishment: The Political Economy of North-Asian Networks (Macmillan; St. Martin's)

Wildlife Tracks 101 (Blackfeet)

Death Walkers

Shamanic Psychopomps, Earthbound Ghosts, and Helping Spirits in the Afterlife Realm

David Kowalewski, PhD

DEATH WALKERS
SHAMANIC PSYCHOPOMPS, EARTHBOUND GHOSTS,
AND HELPING SPIRITS IN THE AFTERLIFE REALM

Copyright © 2015 David Kowalewski, PhD.

All rights reserved. No part of this book may be used or reproduced by any means, graphic, electronic, or mechanical, including photocopying, recording, taping or by any information storage retrieval system without the written permission of the publisher except in the case of brief quotations embodied in critical articles and reviews.

The views expressed in this work are solely those of the author and do not necessarily reflect the views of the publisher, and the publisher hereby disclaims any responsibility for them.

iUniverse books may be ordered through booksellers or by contacting:

iUniverse
1663 Liberty Drive
Bloomington, IN 47403
www.iuniverse.com
1-800-Authors (1-800-288-4677)

Because of the dynamic nature of the Internet, any web addresses or links contained in this book may have changed since publication and may no longer be valid. The views expressed in this work are solely those of the author and do not necessarily reflect the views of the publisher, and the publisher hereby disclaims any responsibility for them.

Any people depicted in stock imagery provided by Thinkstock are models, and such images are being used for illustrative purposes only. Certain stock imagery © Thinkstock.

ISBN: 978-1-4917-7295-9 (sc)
ISBN: 978-1-4917-7294-2 (e)

Library of Congress Control Number: 2015911959

Print information available on the last page.

iUniverse rev. date: 08/10/2015

CONTENTS

Acknowledgements...ix

Introduction...xi

   Near-death experience 1 xi

   The Nearly Forgotten Craft...............xii

   Ghosts on the Move............................xiv

   Outline..xvi

   Near-death experience 2 xix

1 Dead Men Talking...1

   Near-death experience 3 1

   Is There a Paranormal?..........................2

   Are There Discarnate Souls?..................3

   Are Some Discarnate Souls Earthbound?.............5

   Are Psychopomps Needed?....................7

   Death 101 11

2 Who? Where? When?......................................12

   Psychopomp Training 1......................12

   Who 13

   Where...18

   When..22

   Five Risk Factors....................................24

   Psychopomp Training 2......................26

3   Who Benefits? 27

    Grandpa 1...27

    The Unquiet Dead 28

    Survivors..28

    Haunted Parties 30

    Possessed Parties 33

    Near-Death Experiencers 34

    Wider Community 35

    Grandpa 2...36

4   What Psychopomps Do 37

    Déjà vu 37

    Earthbound 37

    Death Rattlers..40

    Have Drum, Will Travel 42

    The Ties That Bind 45

    Wings 1 49

5   Mythic Resources 50

    Wings 2 50

    Hounds of Heaven and More............................51

    Thematics and Symbology 53

    A little birdie 59

6   Trip Planner 61

    Tricksters...61

    Instructional Journeys.....................................62

    Case Selection...63

    Preparing to Journey.......................................67

    Finding Discarnate Souls 71

    Meeting and Greeting......................................72

    Dealing with Problems....................................74

    Escorting 77

    Ethical Guidelines 79

    Lazarus 79

7   Strategies 81

    Goldenrod 1 81

    Logic..82

    The Customer Is Always Right............................83

    Trickery 85

    Bribery..87

    Reunions..88

    Battle 90

    Purpose beyond Self.......................................91

    Attitude of Gratitude 93

    Healing the Wounds.......................................94

    Data Bits..95

    Flattery Will Get You Everywhere.....................95

    Archetypal Resonance.....................................96

    Negotiating...98

    Morbid Humor 99

    Goldenrod 2 100

8   Patterns 102

    The Crying Way 102

    Emotional Bonds 102

    Spirits, Spirits, Everywhere.............................113

    The Crying Way..123

    Energy Body Changes...................................125

    Symbols 127

    Thanks and No Thanks 128

    Timmy...132

9   Real or Make-Believe? 134

    Earthquake..134

    Shake Rattle, and Roll 135

    Other Ways of Knowing 137

    JonBenet 1 143

10 What the Dead Can Teach the Living................144

    JonBenet 2 144

Lessons for Us All 146
Lessons for Survivors 151
Public Policy Implications 153
A Psychopomp Revival? 155
JonBenet 3 157

Appendix: Mythic Allies 159
Chapter Endnotes 167
References 177
About the Author 197

Acknowledgements

Special thanks go to Betsy Bergstrom, Tom Cowan, and Sandra Ingerman for looking at early drafts of the book and offering their wise advice, almost all of which I gladly took and the rest of which I am ignoring only at my own peril. I also thank all those shamanic teachers who brought magic back into my life, and I take full responsibility for any misunderstanding of their instruction. I appreciate especially my psychopomp teachers, who showed me that, while death is not a big deal, dying badly is.

INTRODUCTION

You stay, I go.
    --Ishi, the Yahi native and alleged last Stone Age human, to his friends at his death

Do not disfigure the soul.
    --Druid saying

And each separate dying ember
wrought its ghost upon the floor
        --Edgar Allan Poe, *The Raven*

Near-death experience 1. There I was, a child, hovering above my body that was floating, lifeless, in a swimming pool. As the gods would have it, for reasons I eventually realized, I returned to that body, aware of many things about death that most people have nary a clue about. But it was tough being dead. In addition to the shock and confusion and powerful vibratory "buzz," the shouts of the other kids in the pool assaulted my sense of hearing, the sun blinded my sense of sight, and the chlorine attacked my sense of smell—everything was hyper-real. I was learning first-hand how much the

physical body limits awareness. Later I also realized why ghosts like to hang out in quiet, dark, isolated places like attics and closets and basements, why they prefer coming out at night, and why renovations and demolitions of buildings so rile them up.

Nobody gets out of this life alive, or so they say. Really? True, the body disintegrates, but is that all? Might we in fact "get out alive"? Might our awareness continue? We all know somebody who died. Where did they go, or more basically, what is even meant by "they" and "where"? Can they, do they, interact with us? Might they be stuck in a new version of earthly reality, unable to move on and needing someone to help them do so? Since death is the most universal human experience aside from birth, these are important questions.

Unfortunately, many modern people ignore them, even avoiding any talk of death at all. This book addresses such questions from the shaman-psychopomp perspective, showing how the practice of escorting stuck deceased souls to a state of peace illuminates the profound realities of life, death, and afterlife.

The Nearly Forgotten Craft

Was my near-death experience, described above, the reason I decided to take the shamanic path? According to scientific research, in fact it was very likely. Near-death experiencers return to the earthly realm with special psychic abilities and a wish to serve their people in the helping professions. So when I found out that shamans liberate departed souls and other spirit entities from the earthly realm, I could honestly say, "Bring it on … been there, done that!" Later, when I found out that other near-death experiencers "could communicate with ghosts," I was hooked.

In fact one of the core shamanic practices since ancient times has been the escorting of discarnate souls to the Other Side—psychopomp work. Interaction with the dead has been traced back by some scholars to 30,000 years ago, and by others even further to the Neanderthals. According to one comprehensive survey, "Virtually all spiritual traditions acknowledge some sort of psychopomp." Folklore about the practice is "found throughout the world."

How so? After death, the discarnate soul may or may not move on to a new state of being beyond the earthly plane. If it does in fact "cross over," "move to the Other Side," "go into the Light," it is said to be at peace with itself and the earth it has left. If it does not, it may choose to stay in the earthly realm to help family members and others, and so too be at peace. But other, disturbed souls may still need to work through their psychospiritual dilemmas so as to be free to continue their spiritual journey and so fulfill their soul's destiny. It is these latter souls whom the shaman-psychopomp helps to move on.

But when I tried to find out exactly how psychopomps practice their craft, the literature was scanty and of little help, except for a few notable but limited and outdated exceptions. This was true, even though thanatology may be the world's oldest discipline, and psychopomping one of the most important services that ancient shamans did for their people. I did find a few books, but these were criticized, fairly or unfairly, for the minimal professional expertise of the authors, lack of analysis and synthesis, too few accounts of personal encounters, unsubstantiated claims, and too much irrelevant detail. In brief, psychopomp service had largely disappeared from public view.

Ghosts on the Move

So I figured I had to find out from experience. After many shamanic trainings and journeys to the spirit world, I felt I had reason to speak with some authority on the topic. I also started feeling ahead of the curve. Not only do many people still believe in the afterlife, in the involvement of departed souls in their lives, in psychic powers, and in other mysterious phenomena. They are also tuning in to the paranormal in record numbers. A shamanic renaissance is in full swing, as seen in large gatherings of shamans from around the world. Psychics galore appear on radio and TV talk shows, while websites on the paranormal proliferate.

The media blitz has honored ghosts in particular, as seen in the surprising popular interest in academic books on near-death experiences by experts like Ken Ring. Popular films like *Ghost, Sixth Sense,* and *Ghostbusters* have tracked the popular trend. So too has an amazing number of reality-based TV shows. Of special interest to me was the fictional, but reality-based, *Ghost Whisperer,* an award-winning TV series about a female psychopomp.

What really caught my attention was the interest shown by a growing number of academics in the paranormal, as seen in the increased popular acceptance of scientific findings that document psychic phenomena, and in professional publications like the *Journal of Near-Death Studies, Journal of Scientific Exploration,* and so on. Shamanism in particular is part of this movement, with university courses on the topic, and the appearance of respected publications like *Shaman's Drum, Sacred Hoop,*

Shamanism Annual, Journal of Shamanic Practice, Journal of Contemporary Shamanism, and the like. When a trend gets "campus cred," I know that something important is going on.

Already if you google "shamanism," over a million websites will pop up, and almost one-half million for the closely related "mediumship" and even 0.25 million for "psychopomp." Compare these figures to 1.1 million for Anglicanism, 0.3 million for Methodism, 0.5 million for Presbyterianism, 0.7 million for Episcopalianism, and 0.8 million for Lutheranism. This is not too surprising—the new Christology, for example, increasingly sees Jesus as a shaman.

Interest in the paranormal, especially in shamanism and in particular in psychopomp work, will likely grow. Some 60% of Americans believe in the paranormal, especially the educated. Large percentages of survey respondents claim to have been contacted by deceased loved ones and to be able to communicate with them.

This popular attunement to death and dying is likely to increase as the world's population rapidly ages. As the Baby Boomers of the developed world, and the Green Revolution Boomers of the developing world, approach their final days in the coming decades, the issue of death will become more and more a matter of public discussion. *Without being indelicate, we can say that these Boomers will naturally be thinking a lot about death.* This has already been happening in recent decades, with much talk of "Dr. Death" (Jack Kevorkian), "physician-assisted suicide," "death panels," "living wills," "healthcare proxies," "bereavement counseling," and so on. As the world population "seniorizes," death is rapidly becoming a growth industry in law, medicine, ethics, media, and other fields. The skeletons, so to speak, are prematurely coming out of the closets.

The growing interest in death and dying is also seen in courses on the topic in psychology and other departments at institutions of higher learning across the world. Greatly interested as well are the hundreds of paranormal research teams that have sprung up to document hauntings.

In short, the public is increasingly demanding and consuming information on the most important event in our lives after birth. Shamans, many of whom have had near-death experiences, and who have a background in dealing with the spirit world, may eventually take a seat at the discussion and healing tables. Already hospitals are allowing alternative medical practitioners access to the dying, and shamans are increasingly performing psychopomp service for the departed and their survivors at the time of death.

Outline

That's where I come in—academics are good at writing books, and the world is needing one about the ancient ways of dealing with death. This book, then, illuminates the mysterious worlds of life, death, and afterlife by unpacking the ancient craft of psychopomping while addressing the shortcomings of previous writings on the topic.

Chapters 1 through 3 introduce you to the paranormal, and in particular to ghostly phenomena in the afterlife. Chapter 1 briefly tackles the criticisms that the paranormal is fictional and that spirits don't really exist, get earthbound, or need psychopomps. I bring forth evidence from more than a century of painstaking research on the paranormal that in fact psychopomp work is grounded in reality.

Chapter 2 maps out the personal traits and death circumstances of those persons likely to become earthbound after death, then shows where that binding occurs and when the ghosts are most likely to be activated. From this treatment are extracted five general risk factors for becoming earthbound. For example, the strangeness of the death situation raises such chances, causing souls to wander about, wondering what happened and trying desperately to get back into their bodies.

Chapter 3 addresses the practicality of psychopomp work, listing the beneficiaries and showing exactly how they are helped.

Chapters 4 through 8 present the nuts and bolts of psychopomp work, with many examples from my own experience. These chapters are not meant as a training manual in any way, yet readers who have a special shamanic bent and talent, a formal background and experience in the craft, a calling to do psychopomp work in particular, and special in-depth training in the practice might find them useful. Instead, these chapters are merely meant to describe how psychopomps go about their craft. Chapter 4 lays out the key definitions, topology, and processes associated with the service. While popular attention to death and the afterlife has been a blessing, the curse has been an unclear use of terms like "ghost," "demon," "spirit," "haunting," and so on. This chapter clarifies these terms, then presents initial findings from my own practice.

Chapter 5 excavates the mythic resources of the past that are available to modern psychopomps, noting the spirit allies of many traditions and illustrating the themes and symbols that have empowered the work. Striking cross-cultural similarities around the world, such as symbols of birds and boats, have infused the psychopomp practice of the past and are readily useable by shamans today.

Chapter 6 offers a stylized protocol that summarizes previous psychopomp work. It draws on ancient shamanic principles, as well as specific techniques from around the world and my own experience, that inform the escort process.

Chapter 7 maps out various strategies that psychopomps use to get earthbound souls to cross over, from battling soul abductors to cracking morbid jokes.

Chapter 8 presents the themes that recur in psychopomp journeys, such as the appearance of uninvited spirits and the changes seen in the soul's energy body.

Chapter 9 deals with the possibility that I simply made it all up. I point out how psychopomps, as well as observers, might see that escorting the dead to their next adventure in fact has taken place.

The final chapter brings out the lessons, derived from psychopomping past and present, that we the living can learn from the earthbound dead, for example forgiveness, emotional preparation for death, and not leaving behind a mess for survivors.

The Appendix lists the mythic psychopomp spirits found cross-culturally and treated in chapter 5. Endnotes for chapters, and references, complete the book.

At the beginning and end of each chapter I offer stories from my own life about death, spirits, and psychopomp training. Before starting the book, I asked my helping spirits for guidance. They said, "Tell your stories." Right away I came up with every possible reason not to do that, but they were having none of it: "Tell your stories!" I had no comeback. In fact, ancient shamans regularly narrated their encounters with the spirit world to their people. Also, I had learned not to mock the high-voltage energy of the spirit world. So, I offer a number of such stories, which appear in **boldface type** in the text. Sharp readers will see a thread of destiny weaving its way through the narratives.

Throughout the book, I also present highly abridged cases of my own psychopomp work selected from 93 shamanic journeys I took to escort souls to the Other Side. They appear in *italics* in the text. From this dataset, I offer statistics showing the structure of the journeys, such as the various reasons why souls become earthbound, how often unfamiliar spirits show up during journeys, and so on. Note that you should not attempt such journeys on your own, since not only do they demand general soul-trip skills and years of experience before a high level of competence and comfort is reached, but psychopomping in particular requires specialized instruction. It is not for amateurs. It also calls for a healthy psyche, one well-grounded in everyday reality.

I also give numerous examples from the ethnographic literature on the psychopomping practices of indigenous peoples from around the world, in order to provide a wider context for my own work. Although details vary widely among cultures, certainly a cross-cultural "core" psychopomping service is evident that can be recognized everywhere and that modern shamans can tap into with good effect.

Near-death experience 2. As I hovered above my body that was floating in the pool, the intensity of bodiless

awareness made me want to leave for someplace more comfortable. So I thought of home, and instantly I was there. Later I realized I had traveled, not faster than the speed of light, but out of spacetime altogether. I could go anywhere with simple intent. My soul was truly infinite—without corporeal limitations. Intent, unlike a photon, does not have a material speed limit.

CHAPTER 1

Dead Men Talking

Near-death experience 3. When I first heard about research being done on near-death experiences, I checked out how my own would match. In fact it was validated on all counts but one: I had experienced no life review. I thought maybe the gods had given me a "discount version," but I was dead wrong. As I wondered about it, I realized that I had been so young at the time that I had not made any major life decisions that needed reviewing. So I figured I owed the gods an apology.

Are there really earthbound discarnate souls needing psychopomps? This question breaks down into four sub-questions about (1) the paranormal, (2) discarnate souls, (3) being earthbound, and (4) the need for shamanic escorts to the Other Side.

Is There a Paranormal?

Is there a nonordinary reality beyond our everyday ordinary reality that we can access with what used to be called extrasensory perception but now is called psi? Many modern people have dismissed psi as superstitious "magical thinking" typical of "primitives." Yet that view is fading fast. Some two-thirds of Americans have admitted to such experiences.

Not only have humans experienced the paranormal at least since we came out of the trees, but now we have a century of scientific support for the notion. Rigorous research has evidenced telepathy, clairvoyance, precognition, psychokinesis, spiritual healing, and other paranormal phenomena. Telepathy, for example, which "can take place between discarnate and incarnate spirits," is a perfect example of direct soul-to-soul communication essential to shamanism and now accepted by a significant proportion of scientists.

A number of prestigious research establishments have generated high-quality findings for the paranormal, such as the Stanford Research Institute, Princeton Engineering Anomalies Research Group, and Institute of Noetic Sciences, whose results have appeared in respected publications like *Journal of Scientific Exploration* and *Shift Report.* Recent articles and books offer historical summaries and meta-analyses of this research, all of them urging scientists, many of whom are in denial about psi, to start taking it seriously and not simply write it off as opinion, anecdote, superstition, or hallucination.

Are There Discarnate Souls?

Within the paranormal realm, are there discarnate souls? Are there conscious and intentional energetic entities that once lived on earth but that now exist without any bodies? Does the soul live on beyond death? Is there an afterlife? Do our consciousness and intentionality survive death?

Surely most humans have thought so. Millions throughout the ages and across the world have reported encounters with, even received signs from, the recently departed. Deceased loved ones may appear to a dying person just before the moment of death, a well-documented phenomenon. Survivors may, at the time of the death, experience "electrifying vibrations" at the place where it just occurred. The newly dead may appear to relatives in dreams, which "offer some of the best firsthand evidence of ghosts."

Even in modern cultures an interest in death and the afterlife lives on, and in fact is enjoying a renaissance, as evidenced by the large majority of Americans who believe in the survivability of the soul and an afterlife. In 2009, for example, we learned that only 12 percent of Americans did not believe in life after death. The trend, according to a 2007 survey, has been climbing steadily, a development occurring in many other countries as well. Of course popular beliefs cannot always be trusted, but the solid majorities that consistently assert soul survivability cannot be simply written off.

In fact over a century of evidence supports the notion, and recent scientific research is no exception. Among anthropologists, psychologists, and sociologists who have "gone native," as academic and governmental specialists put it, immersing themselves physically in local cultures to better understand indigenous peoples, many have come back having experienced spirits of some kind.

Comprehensive reviews of the scientific literature clearly point to an afterlife. Surveys show that 30 to 42 percent of respondents say they've felt in touch with someone who died, including 60-90 percent of widows and widowers. Certain "classic" happenings, like falling photographs and familiar aromas, are experienced by many. Afterlife contacts are sensed even by those with limited psychic gifts and may continue for years. Evidential experiences with the dead (ones with ghosts revealing unknown information) and shared ones (ones with two or more witnesses perceiving them) are not uncommon.

People have sensed discarnate souls in various ways, such as "phone calls from the dead." Studies have reported frequent death coincidences, namely strange contacts of some kind with people not known to be ill or dead, at the moment of their passing. Contacts often occur 12 or so hours after the death. Researchers have found cross-correspondences among pieces of information given by spirits to mediums across the world that made no sense separately but did so collectively. Meta-analyses have concluded that enough scientific evidence for afterlife communication exists that it simply cannot be dismissed.

Living humans themselves can experience physical reality from outside of their bodies, namely become "nonlocalized." In quantum physics, nonlocality is an established fact, and its link to the paranormal is more and more evident. Studies of remote-viewing have shown that a living human soul on earth can leave its body and experience physical reality far away in space and time—evidence so compelling that the U.S. government spent millions of dollars developing this "metaphysical technology" for intelligence gathering by "psychic spies."

Evidence from near-death experiences, documented in the *Journal of Near-Death Studies* and elsewhere, is even more telling. Extensive research suggests strongly that consciousness survives death. Despite efforts by skeptics, the near-death experience cannot be reduced to brain chemistry. Some people, in short, have indeed experienced death, becoming discarnate souls, but lived to tell about it. Studies show that, while out of body, near-death experiencers have extremely vivid sense awareness, see dead relatives they did not even know had died, and with the speed of thought travel to distant locales, which upon return to their bodies they can accurately describe.

Are Some Discarnate Souls Earthbound?

Are some of these deceased souls earthbound, namely stuck or lost or trapped somehow, unable or unwilling to move on to their next adventure? Can we get in touch with them? Almost universally people have held this conviction. Certainly "one of the distinguishing features of the ... human," according to paranormal researcher James Overton, "is ... burying our dead and 'communicating' with them, under the assumption that their primary existence lies in ... an 'alternate' reality."

According to one global study, belief in ghosts was found in 65 out of 66 cultures. Some Native-Americans, for example, avoid saying the name of a deceased soul since it may get confused and think it's still alive.

A clear majority of Americans, according to a 2003 poll, believe in ghosts. In 2005 almost 2 out of 5 Americans believed in haunted houses, including well over half of young adults. There has also been a resurgent

David Kowalewski, PhD

interest in possession in recent decades. Hauntings and possessions have been well documented in academic work, as found in the *Journal of Religion and Psychical Research* and elsewhere.

Voluminous "instrumental transcommunication" data from discarnate souls has been evidenced at least since the time of the telegraph. Today's equipment includes multifield meters, ion counters, static meters, data loggers, motion detectors, film and digital and infrared and full spectrum cameras, seismographs, electromagnetic frequency (aka "K-2") meters, thermometers, tape and digital voice recorders, TV sets, telephones, and computers. The data, which cannot be explained by physical causes, include the following.

Sights: foot and hand prints on floors and walls, flashing lights, moving and falling objects, full-body apparitions, words and images on TV screens and computer monitors and fax machines.

Sounds: musical instruments playing, voices, footsteps, rappings.

Touches: scratches and welts and bite marks on the body, shoves, nudges, breezes, static charges like hair standing on end.

Temperatures: cold and hot spots many degrees different from the ambient temperature.

Electromagnetic frequency spikes: inexplicable surges in energy detected on instruments.

Other:

> appliances such as TV sets, and other electrical equipment such as lamp lights, switching on and off by themselves;

doors opening and closing by themselves;

faucets turning on and off by themselves;

motions of objects, and pressings of flashlight buttons, in response to questions;

odd behavior of animals;

communications, often via mediums, of information unknown to observers but later verified by historical records and eyewitness accounts;

personality changes in possessed victims;

vivid nightmares about, or precognitive dream visitations by, a deceased; and

synchronicities.

Also, academics have carried out quantitative investigations of apparitions and other forms of haunting. Often the events are experienced by multiple competent observers at the same time at the same site. But skeptics there often fail to see, or to admit, the phenomena, illustrating the well-known "sheep and goats" effect in paranormal research.

Professional counselors, in fact, have made good use of the reality of ghosts to treat their patients. In short, evidence for a "science of spirits" is a mountain that is rapidly rising but still covered by a rug of denial.

Are Psychopomps Needed?

Many a tie can bind discarnate souls to the earthly realm. But why do they *continue* stuck between the earth and the Light? Why, despite having shed their bodies, do they *keep* an earthly consciousness? Why do they *stay* unwilling or unable to cross over? Why are they *still* active on the earthly plane? Can't they untie their bonds themselves? Do they need a psychopomp?

Traditionally, there have always been some humans specially equipped to escort such souls to the Other Side. Psychopomping, one of the core skills practiced by shamans throughout the ages, has been viewed by our ancestors everywhere as somehow necessary. Certain figurines from ancient burial sites, for example, are believed by some anthropologists to represent the physical postures of psychopomps during their journeys into the realm of the dead. Tibetan Buddhists as well say that compassionate spirits may be needed to help discarnate souls move on. Psychopomps, then, have served deceased souls as ushers, guides, travel companions, healers, and mentors for millennia.

Of course, not everything that humans for thousands of years have held to be true has turned out correct— geocentrism is an embarrassing case in point. But psychopomping is not just an ancient myth. Recent studies have shown the healing power of shamanism, such that the U.S. National Institutes of Health has officially funded research on the tradition. Research too has suggested the need for gifted, trained, and motivated living humans to communicate with the dead. Respected clinicians have documented the spirit-possession of patients and the need for professional clearing of the possessors. So-called "multiple personality disorder"— more recently "dissociative identity disorder"—which failed to win acceptance by practicing psychologists, is increasingly seen as good old-fashioned spirit-possession.

Yet most of the souls that shamans encounter in their psychopomp journeys, in contrast to much of the medium's work, are rather quiet and even pathetic, having little power to affect our ordinary reality and so to get the attention of normal living humans. The souls that do break through are the more powerful ones, but even then, the living humans that they contact are terrified and flee and so are of little help. So, if souls have trouble coming to us, a shaman is needed to go to them.

Psychopomps seem to be needed, too, because usually the newly dead have little experience with nonordinary reality, and so need help in navigating that realm. Earthbound discarnate souls walk in nonordinary reality but not easily in ordinary reality, while most living humans walk in ordinary reality but not easily in nonordinary reality. The shaman-psychopomp can walk easily in both worlds, living both a physical and a metaphysical reality. In short, both the earthbound soul and the psychopomp are closely connected to both realities—ordinary and nonordinary.

Put another way, the soul is stuck to ordinary reality but lives in nonordinary reality, while the psychopomp lives in ordinary reality but can navigate in nonordinary reality. Since the soul is *earth*bound, then, it needs to interact with some living *earthly* human, but since it lives in the *non-earthly* realm, it needs as well to interact with some human accepting and familiar with the *non-earthly* realm. The shaman-psychopomp fits the bill perfectly.

For this reason the shaman is often portrayed as a "walker between the worlds" or a "walker in two worlds," as seen in the self-description of Vodou shamans as "doctors with two heads." Shaman-psychopomps are the only ones, it seems, with the necessary familiarity and skills to do the job.

In some cases as well, the discarnate soul will not believe other deceased souls that it is dead, and instead requires the word of a living human. In other cases, the confused or otherwise vulnerable soul has been captured by other, malevolent spirits, and needs a powerful champion to free them from bondage. Also, the discarnate soul often needs spiritual healing, and shamans have the skills and experience to do that in the nonordinary world of the dead.

Among shamans, those whose initiation was a near-death experience seem especially fit for psychopomp work. Not only are they at ease with the fact of death, but they can be especially skilled at escorting the dead, since they have had vivid personal experience with that realm. Having felt the hand of death directly, they are best able to sympathize with the deceased. Many near-death experiencers, while out of body, have met departed loved ones, and upon return want to revisit nonordinary reality. In particular, the new psychic abilities they returned with enable them to deal with the invisible world of discarnate souls. The near-death experience, it seems, provides ideal "on-the-job-training" for psychopomp work.

To sum up: Yes, there is a paranormal, there are spirits, there are earthbound ones, and there are psychopomps who are needed and willing and able to help.

So it's game over—the skeptics have been routed. Yet they keep repeating that the "extraordinary claims" of the paranormal "demand extraordinary evidence." Here's what's extraordinary: intelligent people refusing to accept the extraordinary amount of evidence about nonordinary reality. This denial is the extraordinary claim, and the deniers need extraordinary evidence to support it.

Death 101. Sitting in a university classroom on the first day of my first philosophy class, I was eager to learn about the meaning of life. But then the professor walked in and announced that we were going to spend the whole semester talking about death. What? So much for the meaning of life! Much later I "got it." It is the meaning of death that gives us the meaning of life. Shamans agree, and might add that the deceased may be even wiser than professors of philosophy.

CHAPTER 2

Who? Where? When?

Psychopomp Training 1. I had to find out more about ghosts—since I had been one myself—so I enrolled in a workshop on death and psychopomp work. I suspected I was on the right track when, the day before the workshop, a dead corvid—the crow family mythically associated with death—showed up on my driveway (more about morbid corvids later). At the workshop's first meeting, the first words out of our teacher's mouth were, "Anybody find a dead bird on their driveway?" Two of us raised our hands—whoa! "It's the universe saying 'This is the real deal,'" he said. "We're not making things up things here." He was dead serious.

Earthbound souls are hardly distributed randomly across the spectrum of deceased persons, places, or times. Instead, certain kinds of persons, places, and times are most likely to display earthbound soul behavior. So, then, who is most likely to be earthbound? Where is such binding most likely to be found? And when are such souls most likely to be activated? Ferreting out these patterns can inform the psychopomp's work to boost its efficiency and efficacy.

Who

Death, contrary to some commentators, is not a huge rupture of consciousness, bringing us bliss, enlightenment, or pearly gates. Humans at death leave their bodies with the same thoughts, feelings, and so on that they had at their last breath. As such, discarnate souls may be earthbound for reasons directly relating to their psychospiritual state at the very time of death.

The following types of souls are most often met by the shaman. Realize that many, if not most, of these souls transit to the Other Side without getting stuck at all. A certain number, though, do get stuck, especially those in multiple such categories.

Children. A disproportionate number of young souls are encountered by the psychopomp. In almost 3 out of 10 of the episodes of my journeys, I met youngsters 12 years-old or younger (29%). This is an amazing statistic, given the fact that youth are the *least* likely age-cohort to die, and so children should be the *least* likely to be found in the realm of the dead by the shaman. Why so many?

Since most children likely assume they are going to live forever, death is not a reality to them, nor is an afterlife. This is especially true if no one close to them has died. In contrast, most elders have had plenty of time to prepare to die and aren't terribly surprised when they do. Also, very young children are in fact living in both ordinary and nonordinary realities simultaneously, for example talking with "imaginary friends," namely spirits.

Upon dying, then, the afterlife on the earthly plane simply looks to them like their earthly life continuing in a non-earthly, namely already familiar, dimension. Finally, parents and children who died together at sites of mass death (accidents, violence, epidemics) will cling to each other, or search for each other if separated, out of affection and dependence.

Addicts. Addicted discarnate souls often feel the need to continue their substance abuse, and may well possess a living addict to do just that. They are still fixated on getting the next "fix"—possibly because that is exactly what they died from.

Sudden death victims. Unexpected, premature deaths, especially highly traumatic ones, are a major cause of being earthbound. Such souls had no time to prepare for death and so are shocked, disoriented, and confused. They had no chance to assimilate the imminent reality of dying. Some of these souls do not realize they are dead or refuse to accept it. These include victims of accidents like a fall from a ladder, drowning, cardiac arrest, and hotel fire. Vehicle and industrial accidents may leave a road, factory, and mine haunted for some time. Train wrecks, plane crashes, and shipwrecks leave earthbound souls behind. Also, natural disasters like earthquakes, tsunamis, floods, volcanoes, avalanches, tornados, and hurricanes generate a spike in reports of hauntings and spirit-possessions. Accounts of such paranormal activity increased dramatically, for example, around New Orleans after Hurricane Katrina.

Homicide victims. Dying a bloody death at the hands of other humans leaves many a soul earthbound. Many of these souls belonged to groups most at risk for such violent deaths, like military units, gangs, prison inmates, prostitutes, and pariah ethnicities. The specific occasions of death may have been robbery, rape, vigilante assault, terrorist attack, mass murder, and warfare. Such deaths are associated with powerful emotions like hate, anger, sexual attraction, and fear—all of which can tie the departed to the earthly plane. Battlefields, for example, elicit many haunting reports. According to one research estimate, apparitions by victims of such violence are almost five times greater than the background rate. Post-traumatic stress disorder, it seems, occurs both before *and* after death.

Suicides. Those who take their own lives may also stay earthbound, since they are not only still in despair, but also in shock and embarrassment that they really didn't "end it all" after all. Lack of faith in a pleasant afterlife or in a higher power leaves them feeling distraught. They may also feel guilty at leaving their survivors "with a mess" and so want to stay around to "set things right." To the extent that the victim, as well as the survivors, have not forgiven the act, moving on is that much more difficult.

Atheists. Imagine not believing in an afterlife, much less a redemptive and forgiving spiritual realm, and then finding yourself there—a psychological shock to be sure. Psychopomps find such souls surprised, embarrassed, confused, and often stubborn about their disbelief in the Light. Some may simply be waiting to go out of existence altogether. Atheism after all is an *ism,* and so its adherents can be just as stubborn, dogmatic, and fundamentalist as believers.

The risk-averse. Those whose earthly lives were full of fear, and so who clung to the familiar, the comfortable, and the risk-less, are rarely ready for a new adventure, especially in a strange and intense reality. Such souls, who were in fact already stuck in ordinary reality, are not ready for nonordinary reality either and so want to get back to their familiar earthly life, afraid to admit that such is, in fact, impossible.

Unexemplaries. Those who led less than honorable lives on earth are also more likely to stick around on that plane, for example sadists, gangsters, torturers, and psychopaths. They may be full of remorse and afraid of a divine justice like "hell." They may want to reform themselves, or feel so much regret that they want to stay connected to earth to make amends, righting the wrongs they visited on the living. They may be seeking forgiveness. They may also believe, because of guilt, that they're unworthy of a pleasant afterlife. Going to the Light, then, seems not a blessing but a curse.

The resentful. Souls who were treated badly on earth may still be bitter towards survivors, for example about the lack of proper funeral rites. In Greek tradition, if deceased souls were not given an honorable rite of passage, they would haunt the living. Resentful souls, too, may have suffered false charges and vile rumors during life and so want to defend and exonerate themselves. They may be revanchists who never forgave because they never healed their wounds, and so feel the need to take out revenge against the living. These souls are often perceived by the living as "demons," but in fact are just indulging in hate, anger, and so on. Some may be obsessed with a living human, even committing, spiritually, the crime of stalking. Souls who died young may be bitter at not having experienced a full earthly life and so want to stick around to do so.

Protectors. Some ethnocentric souls choose to stay on the earthly plane to protect their native people, especially their immediate descendants. This seems to account for the many encounters by living humans with native spirits dressed in their indigenous clothes. Common as well is the soul who stays to watch over loved ones, be they family or friends, as "guardian angels." This is a common pattern, especially in the case of mothers who left very young children behind.

Workaholics. Achievement-obsessed souls may have unfinished business in the earthly realm, which may be something as small as getting the garage roof fixed, to a wider cause like overthrowing a corrupt dictator. These souls, too, may feel guilty at leaving their survivors unprepared for their deaths.

Multitaskers. For Tibetan Buddhists, the discarnate soul may simply lack control over its own consciousness, namely be scatterbrained, inattentive, distracted, and unfocused. Such souls may simply have trouble "getting it together" enough to travel to the Other Side.

Spiritual abductees. Shamans know that a discarnate soul may be held captive by malevolent spirits taking advantage of its lack of character and its negative feelings, especially self-destructive ones like shame and regret. Such emotions form a welcome mat for the dark side, which turns the soul's afterlife into an actual "hell." These malevolent spirits may then persuade or force the soul to do their dirty work. Among the Koryak, for example, an evil spirit can carry off a discarnate soul and prevent it from crossing over. Such spirits are rightfully called "thieves."

An earthbound situation can be made worse, according to some observers, by survivors who cling to the departed soul out of grief, emotional dependence, loneliness, unfinished business, or other reason. The psychopomp, then, may have to heal the living as well as the dead.

Where

When it comes to ghosts, some places are soul-magnets and so form the lore of famous hauntings. Such kinds of sites include the following.

Total institutions. Most modern people live at least part of their daily lives in institutions like a job site or school. But some institutions encompass all or most of a person's basic needs such as food and sleep—what sociologists call total institutions—such as prisons, boarding schools, residential colleges, and leper colonies. The more needs that such institutions provide for their inmates, the more likely they harbor discarnate souls. Inmates dying in such places often know little else, since much of their entire lives, almost every minute of every day, has been spent there. Other examples include sanitoria, labor camps, mental institutions, reform schools, and orphanages. The notoriously haunted North Head Quarantine Station in Sydney, and the Waverly Hills Sanatorium in Louisville, KY, are cases in point.

Such institutions have also housed inmates over several decades and so have witnessed many deaths, and so the mathematical probability of a lot of discarnate souls wandering about in such a small space is high. Excluded here are most convents and monasteries, since inmates have usually led long and exemplary lives during which they've prepared for death on a nearly daily basis and then die peacefully. Normally patients in hospice care facilities also have ample time to prepare for death.

Places associated with addictive substances. People who die as addicts, especially if they need a fix at the time, are drawn to places where such fixes are available, especially their "old haunts" during life, often possessing the patrons to "get high by proxy." Such sites include opium dens, crack houses, bars, taverns, pubs, nightclubs, and dance halls, for example the White Horse Tavern in Newport, RI. Especially if these establishments were associated with violence over time, like Old West saloons and Mafia speakeasies and biker bars, are ghosts found hanging around.

Homicide sites. Ghosts may get stuck at the sites where they suffered torture and violent death at the hands of other humans, such as castle dungeons, jails, battlefields, military ships and bases, and POW camps. The Tower of London, USS Hornet, and Ft. Leavenworth, KS, are good examples. Sites of gangland activities, such as casinos and brothels, harbor ghosts. Locales where homicides occurred are especially likely to be haunted if the deaths were many and unexpected, such as from terrorist attacks and gangland shootouts. Many accounts of ghostly activity, for example, appeared around the site of the World Trade Center in New York City right after the 9/11 events. Other sites of mass killings, like Sabra and Shatila, Wounded Knee, and My Lai, have a similar story. For this reason, some modern shamans travel in ordinary reality to these sites to escort the victims to the Other Side.

Physical care facilities. Clinics and hospitals are locales of many deaths, including those of patients not ready to die, and so are notorious for hauntings. The specific rooms to which the victims of mass homicide, accidents, and natural disasters are brought, such as emergency rooms and operating rooms and morgues, witness many earthbound spirit manifestations. Also, sickness and anesthesia leaves living patients weak, drugged, and unconscious, and thereby vulnerable to possession by such ghosts.

Big old hotels. Tens of thousands of guests have patronized such establishments, and as statistics would have it, a fair number have died. The same might be said of cruise ships. Significant here is that such deaths were almost certainly unexpected—most guests do not check into a hotel, or book a cruise, in order to "check out" of their lives for good. As such, sudden deaths like heart attacks leave the souls disoriented and lost, wandering the hallways wondering what happened. I remember one night when I walked into a hotel hoping for a room, but the receptionist said, "We only have one room left and previous guests have seen apparitions there—do you still want it?" I said, "Are you kidding? Where's the key?!"

Séance locales. Wherever inexperienced metaphysical adventurers open a portal to nonordinary reality by way of Ouija boards and seances and similar rites, without proper training and clear and strong intention, without telling the souls to leave, and without closing the portal afterwards, hosts of ghosts may come uninvited—and stay.

Cemeteries? Much lore about ghosts centers on burial sites. But when I was working my way through college during two summers mowing grass at a large urban cemetery, I got exactly the opposite impression. I had no ghostly encounters, nor did any of my many co-workers to my knowledge. In fact, I found the place peaceful, even uplifting. How so?

{} Many of the deceased have picked out their own gravesite, indicating a preparation for, and resignation to, death and the afterlife, as well as a feeling of peace about the body's locale, so they have likely moved on beyond the corporeal.

{} The earthbound soul normally attaches to the place of the death, not the burial or other funerary locale.

{} Many earthbound souls don't know or won't admit they're dead, so why would they be at a funerary site?

{} There is little human energy at such sites to tap into—the place is "dead."

{} Possessor souls want to inhabit a living body, not a dead one.

{} Some deceased souls stick around to help the living—not the dead.

{} Usually earthbound souls don't have issues with the dead, just with the living.

{} Tombs and gravestones, often bedecked with flowers, bespeak a concern by the living for the dead, so the deceased have little reason to be resentful of the living.

As such, in my experience, discarnates have little emotional resonance with graves.

But there are exceptions. First, some discarnates may accompany their body to the burial site to witness the funeral ceremony and maybe to send a last message to survivors at the grave, or at least "just to see who turned up"! Second, at graves for the dead who have not processed the grief they accumulated throughout life, hauntings may occur. During my cemetery job, I was asked one day to drive across town, with a very small mower, to another cemetery. When I got to the site, I drove several times around an apparent vacant lot surrounded by a dilapidated fence, but saw no cemetery. I finally got out of the truck and walked into the lot—it was a paupers' cemetery, overgrown with weeds, one tiny flat grave marker right next to another, most broken without even a name inscribed. A heavy sadness and grief was overwhelming, even palpable, and within minutes tears were flowing down my cheeks. Clearly the place was haunted, the homeless souls having nowhere else to go. Other exceptions would include burial sites of indigenous peoples, especially if they have been desecrated by colonists, as well as historical cemetery sites where many homicides took place nearby, such as near a battlefield or prison. Gettysburg National Cemetery is a prime example.

When

Earthbound souls are also more active at some times than others.

Symbolically significant events. Manifestations are most likely on dates of special emotional significance. At such symbolic times, interpersonal ties may elicit, for example, apparitions or voices. Special dates like Valentines Day, Christmas, Thanksgiving, and Father's and Mother's Day are good examples. A departed husband, say, may appear to his wife on their wedding anniversary. Symbols, including symbolic times, matter a great deal in nonordinary reality. By paying attention to such dates, the shaman can get an idea of who is doing the haunting, why, and how to deal with it.

Renovations. Building-repair and reconstruction rile up ghosts, who then start to manifest. By disturbing their hideouts with loud noises and bright lights and strange smells, ghosts are likely to react with disturbances of their own. The renovations may literally bring ghosts out of the woodwork. The shaman, knowing this, might do a ceremony of apology to the soul to get in its good graces before escorting it to the Other Side.

Historical reenactments. Re-creating important events, especially violent ones, can easily stir up ghosts. To traumatize already traumatized souls, say at bloody battlefields or massacre sites, is hardly a good way to avoid hauntings. The psychopomp, by knowing the historical period and the particular events that caused the earthbound problem, can then better communicate with the ghosts on their own terms and on the basis of background facts. One such type of reenactment is the old dramatic play, which brings out deceased actors wanting to "star again." For this reason, nocturnal illumination in theatres is called a "ghost light," deliberately left lit for ghosts to act out their parts at night, undisturbed by the living. Grateful ghosts, then, will hopefully not disturb the live performances.

Dreaming. Sleep is an especially propitious time for a ghostly manifestation, yet such a communication is often written off as "just a dream." Yet dreaming, in fact, lies at the very interface between ordinary and nonordinary realities, making it an ideal condition for discarnates in nonordinary reality to communicate with the living in ordinary reality. Sleepers also have no ordinary reality distractions to tie them to an earthly awareness and so are open to a non-earthly one. Dreamtime, then, is a portal between ordinary and nonordinary realities, an ideal time for the dead to contact the living. Such "visitation dreams" are known to be especially vivid and clear in terms of images and sounds and to be easily remembered.

Five Risk Factors

From this survey emerge five broad risk factors that raise the probability of an earthbound soul manifestation. First, *the stronger the emotional bond* of the deceased to any specific earthly object, event, cause, person, place, or time, the greater the probability of attachment after death. In particular, the greater the emotional arousal of the deceased at the very moment of death, the harder the moving on.

Second, *the less chance the soul had to prepare for death*, the greater the likelihood of being earthbound. Sudden, and especially violent, deaths may leave some souls disoriented, confused, and lost.

Third, *the greater the soul's habituation* during life to ordinary realities, especially in the form of addiction, obsession, and fear of any kind of change, the stronger the binding to the earthly plane. A person not free of things during earthly life may be unlikely to be so after it. Note here that we are not talking about a cold lovelessness. True love liberates and empowers, it doesn't cling; a dependent powerlessness is what clings. People who die to everything now don't have to later. For this reason, the wisdom traditions have stressed the importance of nonattachment—not a heartless apathy but a bouncy freedom, like bubbles on the quantum sea.

Fourth, *the greater the indulgence in negativity during life*, the more the deceased soul may fear to move on to possible judgment and retribution. Negative life-styles and feelings like anger and hatred and revenge can be especially obstructive to crossing over.

Fifth, *the strangeness of the surroundings where the death took place* can leave the deceased feeling lost and so increases the likelihood of being earthbound. Such unfamiliarity can cause souls to wander about, wondering what happened and trying desperately to get back into their bodies. This may be the best argument of all for taking the terminally ill out of hospitals to die at home.

These risk-factors give us predictive power about the Who, Where, and When of psychopomp work. First, the Who. Consider two deaths from heart attack, the first occurring after several minor attacks that took place over several years, and the second coming like a thief in the night after a life of good health. The first soul, who had plenty of time to prepare for death, is less likely to become earthbound than the second.

Next, the Where. The most likely site for encountering earthbound souls is surely the prison. This total institution witnesses, over a long period of time, a number of sudden and violent deaths of unexemplary inmates, many of whom were living in anger, revenge, cynicism, and despair about any kind of pleasant afterlife. Many such inmates were addicts, and find it relatively easy to smuggle in their drug of choice. Prison suicides are common, as seen in policies disallowing materials such as ropes that might make such deaths easier. Violence by ethnic gangs, psychopaths, and the mentally deranged is not unusual. The notoriously haunted New Mexico State Penitentiary, which experienced one of the bloodiest prison riots ever recorded, is a case in point. As such, not only is prison a toxic situation in itself, but being haunted by former prisoners makes it doubly so. Inmates, staff, and visitors can all be at risk.

Finally, the When. Suppose a family experiences a home haunting on Christmas Eve, a time of special emotional symbolism to the haunter. If they ask the

David Kowalewski, PhD

cleric of a bureaucratic religion to "bless" or "clear" the place, or a paranormal research team to investigate it, the ghost often becomes even more active. Without an understanding of shamanism, in particular the need to do background work on the situation and respect the feelings of the haunter, such requests almost always just disturb the ghost more, making matters worse.

So, if you don't want to get possessed, then avoid drinking at an old Mafia hotel bar, going on a tour of Alcatraz or the Alamo, and participating in historical reenactments at Gettysburg. (No problem, thank me later.)

Psychopomp Training 2. The workshop teacher divided our class into pairs of students to track each other's soul in nonordinary reality during shamanic journeys, then started drumming. My partner took off on her soul-trip, while I stayed behind trying to keep bioresonant with her spirit until I was given the go-ahead to start tracking her. At the signal, I started trailing her with the help of Crafty Canine, my helping spirit who, nose to the ground, tracked her energy body up to and through a house, whose front door was open but whose back door had been shut. We then trailed her to a treetop and then to a cave, but then I had the feeling she had left and gone back to the house, to which I felt strongly drawn. Afterwards, during our debriefing, she told me that my route was exactly the one she had taken. "I can do this," I said to myself, "I can track souls in the unearthly realm." I felt like asking the spirits, "Do I get a raise now?"

CHAPTER 3

Who Benefits?

Grandpa 1. I had always been close to my grandfather. When he was in a nursing home during his last days, I used to visit and play pool with him, which he greatly appreciated. So I was especially sad when he passed. A few days after his funeral, I was standing next to a wall in my apartment where I had hung a photograph that a friend of mine had taken of an old man who reminded me of Grandpa. As I was standing next to the photo and thinking about how much I missed him, it suddenly fell off the wall.

Shamans have long provided practical services for their people, such as finding animals for the hunt and healing the sick. In such cases we clearly see that, if the shaman fails, dire consequences may follow.

With respect to certain other shamanic skills, though, the link between practice and practicality seems more tenuous. Why should anybody care, really, if someone has lost a soul part? Is society really worse off? Such questions can, in fairness, be asked in particular about psychopomp work. To modern humans, it has a very low or non-existent priority, since its usefulness seems hardly clear and concrete.

But this view is short-sighted. Below I map out the utility of psychopomp work for discarnate souls, survivors, haunted and possessed parties, near-death experiencers, and the wider community.

The Unquiet Dead

Many discarnate souls are bound to the earthly plane because of unfinished business with the living—a problem the psychopomp can help resolve by simply providing information. In other cases, the shaman can heal the soul from grief, anxiety, fear, confusion, guilt, grudge, and even a personal "hell" resulting from a less than exemplary life. Some souls who suffered a violent and unexpected death may simply be confused about being dead, or refuse to admit it. Some may need a soul retrieval to regain the spiritual integrity and vitality to move on. Others are simply lost or disoriented in the discarnate realm and need a guide.

As a result of the psychopomp's efforts, the soul can then fulfill its purpose in its "next life," whatever that may be. Shamans offer nothing less than counseling for the dead. Psychopomp work, in short, effects the changes needed by the soul to get past its earthbound state and resume its journey of evolving to greater wisdom and power.

Survivors

The survivors of the discarnate soul also benefit. Deaths of spouses and other close family members have long ranked at the top of major life stressors. The ghosts of our ancestors, it is said, can visit their problems on us, their descendants. Departed kinfolk can become "hungry ghosts" seeking revenge. In the Peruvian Q'ero tradition, deceased "vagabond souls" can make living persons sick. The Navajo say that one can become ill simply from proximity to dead souls. Among the Washo, the belongings of a deceased were burnt so the ghost would be unable to retrace a path to the physical world. Boniwa shamans in Brazil teach surviving relatives special chants to protect them from departed souls.

So, sensing ghosts of loved ones may seem exciting and exotic, and offer some comfort in the short run, but in the long run is not necessarily a good thing at all. Stuck dead souls can leave living souls stuck. According to one study of widows' encounters with their deceased husbands, not only did those reporting a negative experience have greater difficulty coping with their loss, but those reporting a positive one did so as well. The psychopomp, by guiding the soul to a state of peace and sharing that event with survivors, can shorten their grieving process since they will no longer feel obliged to continually deal with, and be reminded of, the deceased. By healing the dead, the psychopomp heals the living from their grief. The shaman helps survivors achieve closure, so that they themselves can move on to their own next adventure. This, in turn, has positive health effects. One might say, then, that the shaman brings the living back to life.

Psychopomps are also known to bring back last goodbyes and other useful information from the discarnate soul to its loved ones. Examples include reports on where valuables are hidden or lost or misplaced, and why the soul had to do something that unfortunately caused survivors discomfort.

David Kowalewski, PhD

Haunted Parties

In traditional cultures the most careful attention to dying, death, and the departed has normally been paid. Souls are said to wander about restless if not given proper last rites. Disturbed discarnate souls are believed to cause significant disruption to the living, which is why across the world survivors have tried to placate potentially "hungry ghosts" with elaborate funeral rites, burial mounds and cemeteries, soul houses, remembrances like Tomb Sweeping Day and Day of the Dead, spirit plates of food, altars in the home, and so on. In North and Central Asia, a shaman is sometimes invited to funerals to prevent the deceased from coming back; the Yakut, for example, go to great lengths to prevent the soul of the dead from returning home.

Modernity, though, with its scientism and materialism and secularism, and in particular its skepticism and cynicism about the afterlife and even the existence of the soul and the paranormal, has led to the neglect and even persecution of shamans and, as a result, to their near-disappearance. As a result, according to reports from around the world, the earthly plane has become awash with unquiet discarnate souls who purposely disturb the living.

Discarnate souls with a selfish or harmful intent may become spiritual parasites on the living through a haunting (attachment to a place or object) or possession (attachment to a person). Among the Inuit, for example, ghosts are said to steal the soul of a living person when they fear crossing over alone. In Japan some ghosts are known to take revenge for bad treatment they received while alive by visiting on others similar misfortunes. In

North America, reports of hauntings and possessions have increased as of late.

A discarnate soul may harass the living through hauntings. Victims suffer countless problems, from the physical and psychological to the social and financial. Physical maladies are common. Haunting spirits can damage body and property—not all ghosts are "Casper-friendly." Attacks may include scratches, bruises, and the like. Victims lose sleep because of bodily assaults and fear. Other problems, such as nausea, headaches, and suffocation, can manifest.

Psychological sufferings too are felt. Haunted parties experience not only fear but also stress, which has been linked to depression, memory loss, insomnia, and mood swings. As a result, stress can impair performance at school and job, induce excessive use of drugs, and provoke spousal and child abuse. Psychological problems also follow from the many physical problems stemming from stress.

Since some ghosts, freed from the limitations of the body, can emit powerful energies in a place, a resident can feel the same emotional turmoil as they do. Such atmospherics can cause anxiety, fear, sadness, grief, anger, and similar disturbing emotions. Depression and (possibly justifiable) paranoia, too, can result from the presence of unquiet spirits.

Skeptical victims may experience pseudopsychosis (the false belief they are "going crazy"). They may even commit themselves voluntarily to treatment in a psychiatric hospital. Mentally unstable victims may be pushed to psychic breakdown or suicidality.

If parents and others with authority over a haunted party believe that the victim is truly unstable psychologically, they may order "treatments" like psychotherapy, psychopharmaceuticals, and psychiatric internment, which in turn entail financial costs, physical and psychological side-effects, disruption of job and school life, and social stigma. Children are especially vulnerable, since many are fearless about, and especially attuned to, spirits ("imaginary friends" to most adults). The very young, not yet socialized into skepticism, see and tell their caregivers about a discarnate soul, for which they may be misdiagnosed as delusional or developmentally handicapped, which in turn can lead to unnecessary and expensive "treatment." In rare cases, the state may remove children from their homes. Few people consider hauntings a public health threat, but they are.

Social costs are also evident. Haunted families may split between believers and nonbelievers in the ghost, with resulting conflict. Other social stressors can arise. When discarnate souls secretly move objects in a home, for example, family members may be accused of trickery, carelessness, or theft. In extreme cases, family life can be totally turned upside down. The haunted may suffer alienation and isolation from family, friends, classmates, and neighbors, who curb their association with the "lunatic" or the "witch."

Financial costs can also be incurred. The haunted and their loved ones may feel forced to sell their home at a loss. The selling process itself entails the costs of fees as well as time and energy. Haunted family members may be forced to quit their jobs, or be fired, because of absenteeism, erratic behavior, or residential change.

Hauntings of businesses can also cause problems. Ghosts can stress out security guards, result in lost work time or resignations by valued employees, and force the hiring of new personnel. Spooked customers may avoid haunted hotels, theaters, and restaurants. The hauntings may cause enough financial distress to force a closure.

Possessed Parties

A discarnate soul may also disturb the living by attaching to their bodies. It may want the illusion of still being alive, and so intrude into a victim's consciousness, causing confusion and psychic conflict. It may come in dreams, including nightmares, disrupting sleep with its own agenda. It may also come through outright possession in everyday life, taking control for long periods. The possessor can even change a victim's mind.

Alcohol and drug abusers are often targets of a disturbed spirit, since the victims lack power in many respects and so are vulnerable to takeover, and since they may well share the possessor's own craving and habits. The possessed in turn often do self-destructive things, leading to lost jobs, broken relationships, and other painful disruptions. A possessor may visit its own antisocial behavior onto victims, even trying to get them to commit murder.

The possessed is likely to be misdiagnosed by psychiatrists as having multiple personality disorder or schizophrenia, with the consequent expense, confusion, and disruption of daily life. Worse, "therapy" based on such misdiagnosis may well try to *integrate* rather than *remove* the intrusion, to convince the victim to *accept* rather than *reject* it, with potentially negative consequences.

A psychopomp, then, by freeing the unquiet discarnate soul from its obsession and helping it to move on, is able to heal both the disturbed soul and the haunted or possessed victim at the same time.

Near-Death Experiencers

The psychopomp can also be useful to near-death experiencers. The happening is the most traumatic event one can undergo and live to tell about. Indeed, whereas some near-death experiencers during the episode are welcomed by deceased loved ones, others find no such souls around to "meet and greet" and help them navigate the new strange realm of the dead, and so must face the reality alone with confusion and fear. Also, a few feel a personal "hell" of some kind in the discarnate reality.

Upon returning to their bodies, near-death experiencers often find it hard to share their feelings or, if they do, are not believed about their walk in nonordinary reality. For example, many see the happening as a sacred event and don't want it ridiculed. The predicament, in turn, can add social isolation and even insult and ostracism to their personal trauma. In fact studies have found near-death experiencers feeling alienated, ridiculed, pathologized, and depressed, while expressing a need for mentors, counselors, and psychospiritual guides to help them integrate their experience. As a result, they tend to become invisible, and so those who have never had such an experience are deprived of knowledge about life's most important moment.

Psychopomps, by reporting their soul-trip journeys into the realm of the dead, including encounters with the dark side, can encourage public discussion about death and dying, and so especially help and validate near-death experiencers, who in fact (temporarily) died. Such is especially likely if the psychopomps have had near-death experiences themselves, which is often the case for shamans.

Wider Community

The public can also benefit. "The shaman's task," wrote Trisha Lepp, an expert on psychopomps, "is essential to societal welfare." Psychopomps make us think about the possibility of an afterlife. By bringing back information from the deceased that only the family or other loved ones know about, and by dehauntings and depossessions that result in immediate ends to disruption, they support the notion of the soul's survival. In such ways the living can have a more balanced view of death, viewing it as an important transition and not just a loss. Such acknowledgement can be especially comforting to healthcare workers who agonize over "losing" patients.

By reducing the incidence of hauntings, psychopomps provide a useful public service. Highways haunted by deceased accident victims, for example, can cause additional accidents when drivers see ghosts, thereby putting stress on police and emergency services. Police are also called upon to investigate reported break-ins at haunted houses, worksites, and other structures where "things go bump in the night," but of course most likely lack the shamanic skills to help. Time and taxpayer money are thereby wasted, and community security is compromised. Police may also benefit if psychopomps receive information from discarnate souls to help solve crimes or find missing persons.

Communities can also save resources targeted for the addictions, abuses, psychiatric turmoil, and other problems of haunted and possessed victims who are healed by psychopomps. The costs of law enforcement efforts, emergency room visits, rehabilitation and counseling services, and the like might be reduced in communities with shamans proficient at psychopomp work.

Given the aging population of the world, psychopomps can aid the growing numbers of dying patients in nursing homes, hospices, and hospitals, since they have discoursed with discarnate souls and may in fact, if they are near-death experiencers themselves, be able to share exactly how it feels to die. Thus the psychopomp can best prepare the dying for their next adventure, especially at the moment of transition.

Grandpa 2. When a good friend of mine died, I visited his family to help out. As I was leaving and telling his wife goodbye, a crow suddenly dived and flew right over my head. I could hear the whooshing of its wings just a few feet away. A morbid corvid was visiting me again, this time thanking me for caring about my friend's survivors. And the kicker? My friend had been the photographer who took the picture that reminded me of Grandpa and fell off the wall.

CHAPTER 4

What Psychopomps Do

Déjà vu. During a workshop on psychopomp work, the teacher told us to take a break, and then come back to take a shamanic journey to guide some earthbound souls to the Other Side. As soon as I walked out of the building, a crow suddenly dived and flew right over my head. I could hear the whooshing of its wings just a few feet away.

Everyone has heard of the discarnate soul—the conscious and intentional entity who formerly held together the atoms of a body on earth, but who died and began a new existence independent of a body. Normally imperceptible to incarnate humans on earth, still such a soul may interact, physically and metaphysically, with us by way of apparitions, dreams, and the like.

Earthbound

After death, these "undead dead" may or may not move on to a new state beyond the earthly plane, namely the Other Side. If they do—an event for which there are many terms such as "crossing over," "moving on," and "going through the Light"—they are said to be at peace with themselves and the earth they have left behind. They are no longer earthbound.

But other souls do not move on, remaining earthbound. They are no longer encased in a human body in ordinary reality, but yet are still bound to the earthly plane of nonordinary reality (or to put it another way, still bound to the spiritual aspect of earthly reality). Some choose to stay in the earthly realm to help and protect their families and others, that is, to bind themselves voluntarily to that realm before moving on, and so too are at peace.

But other, disturbed souls may be earthbound out of necessity. Some need to work through their psychospiritual dilemmas so as to be free to continue their souls' journeys. Other souls may be captured and held by discarnate thieves or kidnappers. Souls in such earthbound states are commonly called "trapped," "lost," or "stuck." It is these disturbed and stuck souls the shaman-psychopomp helps to move on.

Such trapped souls are unable to go to the Other Side, namely a state of peace, sometimes called the Source. I like to call that state the Creative Void whence we all came, which is reached by going through the Light, a loving and inviting angelic presence. The Void is not nothing, but a state of being to which souls need to return, their ultimate destiny, in order to continue their evolution. I see it as a cosmic ocean of possibilities, a conscious and intentional "quantum sea of creative energy" from which all things emanate.

The intentionality of earthbound discarnates, then, is still towards the earth and not the Other Side, towards some version of their old earthly life and not towards the afterlife. They are unwilling or unable to turn towards the Light. They inhabit a spiritual dimension, which I sometimes call a "spiritual waiting room" and which Barry Eaton, an afterlife researcher, calls a "halfway house," before they move on. Christians might equate this state to a kind of limbo or purgatory, and Buddhists to a kind of bardo. Whatever the name, souls who are trapped are suffering beings in some way, and the psychopomp is the one who helps relieve their discomfort and guides them through the Light.

So, envision an astronaut orbiting earth whose gaze is narrowly fixated on the planet and who finds it impossible to turn around and see the beautiful stars above. The shaman-psychopomp is the one who helps the astronaut turn around and go back to Source. This sounds easy but, as we know, the devil is in the details. In such cases, shamans need to act as professional "soul-doctors," those who treat the spiritual aspect of maladies, healing the disturbed soul. Psychopomps, then, conduct deceased souls to a state of peaceful contentment. They are liberators, freedom fighters, unbinding the soul from the ties that keep it fastened to the earthly plane.

Note, though, that even long-time and expert shamans will differ on certain features of the afterlife realm. Differences can be seen with respect to how long the soul stays around and if so where, what the Light is, and so on. This is not surprising, since each shaman has a personalized toolkit with its unique nonordinary topography, symbology, helping spirits, ceremonies, strategies, protocols, and style. Many collective differences, too, are observable across cultures. What is important is that practitioners be absolutely authentic during their experiences. Nonordinary reality, after all, is *nonordinary*.

Death Rattlers

Psychopomp work has been has been one of the core practices of shamans throughout the ages. In fact, such work has always seemed natural for shamans, who are typically initiated by some sort of death-rebirth process, such as a dismemberment-rememberment journey. Some in fact are initiated by the near-death experience itself. Perhaps not surprisingly, then, near-death experiencers have been found to come back to their bodies with a lesser fear and a greater acceptance of death and a stronger belief in the afterlife. They also exhibit psi powers like telepathy, clairvoyance, and healing—skills especially useful for dealing with earthbound souls.

Also, shamans are adept at navigating the metaphysical realm, including that of the discarnate soul, in their out-of-body, otherworldly journeys to nonordinary reality to help their people. For example, they journey to retrieve soul parts of the living that have been lost from trauma, to restore power animal protectors, and the like. By means of drumming, rattling, chanting, ingestion of psychoactive substances and so on, they enter an altered state of consciousness, taking a "soul-flight" into a different dimension from the physical, outside of spacetime, namely into nonordinary reality, to gather visual and other data. They are soul-trackers and soul-guides. During the psychopomp journey, the shaman communicates telepathically with the souls and other spirits and sees clairvoyantly what is going on. Thus the shamanic journey—an out-of-body "soul-trip," also called "astral travel" or "remote-viewing"—is closely analogous to the near-death experience. So it is appropriate that shamans are willing and able to guide discarnate souls in the realm of the dead.

Even where bureaucratic religions have overlapped with shamanism, locals have stubbornly clung to the shaman's role of guiding souls to the Other Side. And for good reason. Not only is the work one of the oldest spiritual practices. As psychologist Richard Noll noted, "[It] is an important one in all shamanic cultures. Souls are considered pathogens that cause disease and death if they do not leave the human world and complete their passage to the other world."

Even bureaucratic religions have clung to the psychopomp notion in various ways. Tibetan Buddhists say that spirits may help the discarnate soul move on. Christians assert that the angel Gabriel escorted Mary at her assumption into heaven. Jesus after his death is said to have comforted deceased souls in Sheol. Muslims claim that the angel Gabriel escorted Muhammed on his heavenly journey.

Shamans do not work alone, but engage the services of helping spirits—otherworldly allies—such as power animals and spiritual teachers. Such aides are invaluable for all shamanic services, but especially for psychopomp work, because of the oftentimes confusing and hostile world of the earthly plane of nonordinary reality. Such helpers are especially useful for escorting large groups of discarnate souls, such as those clustering around disaster sites. In the following chapters, my personal helping spirits during psychopomp journeys I will call Crafty Canine, Morbid Corvid 1 and Morbid Corvid 2, Beautiful Warrior, and Native-American. Occasionally I use other spirits, invited or uninvited, for help in the work.

In this other, nonordinary, reality psychopomps may also meet other spirits like shamans who arrive at the scene, deceased loved ones of the discarnate souls welcoming them to the Other Side, and nonhuman entities like angels and demons who are helpful or harmful to the work.

The shaman may also see radiant lights and colors in the deceased's energy body (aka "etheric" or "astral" or "spiritual" body, the "luminous egg," and the "human energy field"). The notion of the energy body goes way back. Roman writers, for example, spoke of death as the process whereby the "spirit body" separates from the physical one. Near-death experiencers also describe it as a body, but one with special powers compared to the physical one it left behind. Today it also has a scientific cachet, being detected several feet from the physical body by means of sophisticated technology, so it is hardly surprising, for example, that some hospital staff see dying patients bathed in a golden glow.

Have Drum, Will Travel

In the following chapters, I offer a number of *highly abridged* accounts of my own journeys, including the name of the place to which I took my soul-trip, the date or period of the death(s) of the discarnate soul(s), the event(s) causing the deaths, and the activities of the psychopomp process. Right after each journey I recorded the happenings to preserve details. At least three days separated each journey from the previous one in order to minimize the boredom-induced "decline effect" well-known in paranormal research.

Note in these cases that I am journeying to the spirits' realm, not vice-versa as in a typical mediumship case.

Whereas a medium usually deals with a soul who has come to ordinary reality from nonordinary reality, the journeying shaman goes from ordinary reality to the soul in nonordinary reality. That is, I am not working via my physical body on-site where the soul has broken through into ordinary reality (say at a haunted house), but instead am traveling in a "soul-flight" to the spiritual aspect of the physical site where the deceased is earthbound, which is usually at or near the place of death. There I work within the nonordinary aspect of those earthly sites, their metaphysical side so to speak. You might call this journeying work then, "long-distance psychopomping."

So the "feel" and character of the cases I describe below are usually quite different from the dramatic scenes of popular "ghostbuster" accounts, where it is the souls who come into our physical realm, rapping on walls and hurling dishes off shelves. The scene of the shaman's journey into nonordinary reality is usually subtler, softer, quieter, and especially far more fluid, such that literally anything magical can happen. Objects may appear which to both the shaman and the discarnate souls are just as vivid as material objects in ordinary reality. For example, in some of my journeys a helping spirit, Crafty Canine, brings a Magic Sled, which to those at the scene is just as real as a wood-and-metal one. Spirits also appear in any form they choose, and quickly morph—shapeshift—into another. In some shamanic trainings I've attended, for example, people have met powerful spirits manifesting as cartoon characters like Wily Coyote.

Nonordinary reality is the timeless realm, such that past, present, and future can easily flow in and out of each other like moving colored liquids in a glass. It is also the spaceless realm, such that awareness can move from one place on the earth to another with the speed of intent. Nonordinary reality, in other words, snaps the arrow of time into three pieces, and grinds the three dimensions of space into dust, then tosses it all to the winds.

The events in the journeys, then, are not fictional in any sense, but are actual happenings in a different reality from the ordinary. Nonordinary reality, in short, is simply very real, more intensely real, and definitely more symbolic and unpredictable, to those engaged in it than is ordinary reality. Shamans don't deal in fantasy, they deal in reality, a deeper reality, a hyper-reality. They may indeed be "fantasy-prone," as some psychologists have labeled them, but that fantasy is full of reality. *Nonordinary reality is a world of magical realism—it's the real deal, just magically so.*

To the uninitiated, untrained, and inexperienced, then, these accounts may strain credulity. Yet I embarked on these psychopomp journeys only after taking well over 800 extended and documented journeys with my helping spirits for other purposes (divination and the like) and regularly producing verifiable results consistent with their intents and useful to my clients.

Some research, in fact, has shown that "imagination" can "induce measurable field effects," influencing cell metabolism and the like. "[I]mages generate frequencies that modify those of the [universal] field, thus achieving the same effects as if the imaged thing were real," wrote psychologist Massimo Citro. "[W]e might not need things anymore if we could recreate the frequencies … [b]y imagining them" since "frequencies emitted with visualization … break the laws of physiology." Also, experienced meditators, with their eyes closed and simply *envisioning* the observation of photons going through a slit apparatus, can collapse the wave function such that light behaves like particles. Perhaps as Einstein pointed out, then, imagination really is more important than knowledge. Or as famous cosmologist Andrei Linde asked, "What if our perceptions are ... even more real ... than material objects?" Reality, then, as paranormal researcher Dean Radin put it, may actually be "built out of imagination," such that imagination *"literally shapes matter"* and therefore "the imaginal and the real are not as separate as they seem." In short, strange things happen in nonordinary reality that don't happen in ordinary reality—*that's why it's called nonordinary*. But still it's reality.

Also, the key tools of the psychopomp, especially telepathy and clairvoyance, have been amply demonstrated in paranormal research. Moreover, the events of my journeys are consistent with the findings of afterlife researchers Bill and Judy Guggenheim, who noted that "neither time nor space are ... limitations for our deceased." Further, happenings that may seem odd even to the psychopomp can in fact be full of meaning to the discarnate soul's survivors upon disclosure.

The Ties That Bind

But why specifically are some discarnate souls earthbound, remaining between the earth and the Light? Many afterlife researchers like Bruce Moen have struggled with the "various reasons [why] people get stuck after death [that] are not fully understood." Further, how prevalent is each? What might the psychopomp beginner expect to find?

In my shamanic journeys I've encountered a wide array of emotional ties that bind the discarnate soul. It is these bonds that the psychopomp is tasked to cut and thereby to free the souls so they can move on to their next adventure in order to evolve to greater wisdom and power.

From my own set of 93 psychopomp journeys, I calculated the frequencies of these ties in order to find their structure. Some of the journeys—9%--had multiple episodes, namely encounters with more than one unrelated individuals or groups, usually at sites of mass deaths. In such journeys, psychopomps may have to take soul-trips around nonordinary reality like soccer moms, using many helping spirits and accumulating what I call "spiritual frequent flyer miles." In all, the journeys involved a total of 106 episodes in which I encountered 205 souls of both sexes, all ages, and several religions in many countries of the world. I deliberately took a cross-cultural approach in order to lower the odds that the accounts are ethnocentric, culture-bound to the Western context, and thereby to raise the odds of uncovering a universal or "core" set of human experiences.

The causes of death were many. Human violence (murder, gangland shootouts, genocide, repression, revolution, war, invasion) was the occasion in 58% of the journeys, a natural disaster (earthquake, tsunami, typhoon) in 28%, a natural cause (sickness, old age) in 9%, and an accident (vehicle crash, drowning) in 5%.

For each specific motive for staying earthbound, I calculated the percentage of episodes in which it was found. In some episodes the individual or group had multiple motives, such as both shame at earthly life and fear of the afterlife.

The literature and popular lore about ghosts stress the ethically tainted reasons for staying earthbound, such as hatred, revenge, and guilt. But common too, I found, are strongly affective, albeit sometimes unrealistic and even futile, motivations for not crossing over. Usually, in fact, such cases proved tougher to resolve than the less benevolent ones, maybe because—ironically—love even in its confused form is in fact a very powerful bond. I encountered such affective reasons for staying earthbound quite often (53% of the episodes), compared to the somewhat more frequent non-affective ones (76%).

The affective ties fell into two categories: (1) a fixation on continuing some public struggle, fight, or cause (16% of all the episodes) and (2) anxiety about finding missing loved ones or fear about leaving them behind uncared for (37%). The first category involved groups like political party factions and military units. The second category involved many kinds of groups, including parents concerned for children or vice-versa (12% each), spouses or partners or lovers (8%), work-mates (colleagues, fellow soldiers) (4%), and pets (1%). So, such affective cases might involve persuading a political demonstrator killed by police to pursue his cause from the Other Side, or enlisting a helping spirit to look after a deceased mother's surviving child so she can cross over.

The non-affective ties fell into many categories. Absent, surprisingly, were jealousy, envy, greed, avarice, and miserliness, although the dataset may have been too small to detect such motives. Capture of the soul(s) by other deceased souls was involved in 2% of all the episodes. The rest of the ties were a very mixed bag of no less than 10 specific feelings. Most common was despair (15%), a theme encountered by other psychopomps. Such cases entailed feelings like preoccupation with one's own suffering, depression about one's miserable way of dying, dread at not being forgiveable, lack of faith in a better

David Kowalewski, PhD

place, disbelief in anything beyond the earthly plane, disappointment at life's failures, and dejection and disgust at the corruption of the bureaucratic religions they had believed in.

Next in rank was confusion (11%), usually stemming from not knowing one was dead or not understanding how one could be dead. Quite common here were cases of very young souls, who had been living in a very "imaginary world" already, and so saw little difference between ordinary and nonordinary realities.

Close behind was shame at something the soul had done or not done (9%), which included embarrassing feelings, humiliation, and anxiety at facing family or friends or workmates on the Other Side. A typical such case involved female souls who had been victimized by sexual violence. A sense of unfairness about the circumstances of death, or at the very plight of being dead, was also common (8%), and often included regret at not having lived long enough, or at not having accomplished what one wanted to achieve in life. Teens and young adults especially felt an injustice at dying so young without having had a chance to live a full life. Revenge and guilt were also met (7% each), as were anger and hatred (5% each). Fear of the afterlife and grief completed the list (5% each), the fearful being anxious about the unknown Other Side or simply clinging desperately to an old good life, and the grieving being held down by the weight of their old life or exhausted from trying to take it with them.

Note that these percentages should not, in any way, be taken as authoritative figures and blindly generalized. They are simply the findings of one practitioner. Other psychopomps, with their unique journey sets, will almost

48

certainly arrive at a somewhat different statistical picture. For example, a nurse shamanizing in a hospital emergency room will likely encounter many victims of suicide, and so get a higher frequency for the despair motive. At the same time, however, the percentages from my journeys are consistent, in rough measure, with other accounts about earthbound souls from across the world and across the ages. As such, they might serve as a baseline to which other practitioners might compare their work.

Wings 1. During one of my classes on shamanism, the teacher gave each of us a piece of soapstone and told us to carve an effigy, a power object, to help us in our work. My piece was already somewhat in the shape of a wing, so I decided to go with that. I was starting to recognize a synchronicity when I saw one.

CHAPTER 5

Mythic Resources

Wings 2. It was the final day of my vision quest, and I was staying up all night before my long-awaited grand-slam breakfast. It was pitch black outside. Suddenly, at 1 a.m., I sensed a huge presence behind me, at which time I felt the brush of a wing against the back of my shoulders. Fast forward a year—the same situation. Just in case "I hadn't gotten the first memo," I sensed a huge presence behind me, at which time I felt the brush of a wing against the back of my shoulders. Years later, I was gratified to read the description of a vision quest taken by Michael Harner, Director of the Foundation for Shamanic Studies, who was awakened one night by a wing brushing across his face.

By definition, shamans work with their own personal helping spirits, each of which assists in one or more particular tasks like divination and healing. Less recognized, however, are helping spirits who have been used for millennia by shamans of particular cultures for a particular task, or what might be called "specialist spirits" of an ethnic group who live on in its myths. Knowledge of such ancient cultural spirits who deal with departing and departed souls can be very useful to the modern psychopomp.

Hounds of Heaven and More

As Michael Harner, the world's foremost authority on shamanism, noted, "Mythology is what's left after shamans die." That is, before civilization appeared, shamans narrated their soul-flight journeys in full detail upon return to their people, and such stories lived on in the tribe's lore. "Probably a large number of epic ... characters," wrote mythologist Mircea Eliade, "were borrowed from ... shamans describing their ... journeys ... to the superhuman world." Many myths, then, are in fact shamanic remnants, or at least "show traces" of primordial shamanism.

As agriculture pushed out hunting and gathering, pagan priests pushed out the shaman and, being less experienced and familiar with navigating nonordinary reality, gradually turned the shaman's personal helping spirits into distant gods and goddesses. Over thousands of years, then, the first accounts of the shaman's spirits were subjected to many changes, so that now it is difficult to separate the original narratives from today's mythological ones. Yet, shamans with their wisdom and power were so important to a tribe that, after they died and even after hunting and gathering was largely displaced, it took great care to recount their soul-trip journeys again and again as accurately as possible lest its world fall apart. So, enough of the original stories remain that today's shamans can learn about early shamanic practice from the later mythology.

Further, cross-cultural similarities in mythic lore, especially about psychopomping, certainly suggest common shamanic roots reaching deep into the past. As such, the myths tell us something about what a typical psychopomp journey might look like during the pre-civilizational era.

Mythology, then, can show today's shamans something of how it was done in the old days, offering them a window onto truly ancient conceptions and practices, despite losses to the mists of time and alterations of the originals due to faded memory, artistic license, and syncretism. Pagan lore, in short, can allow modern psychopomps not only to get in touch with the same spirits used in ancient shamanism, but to use its themes and symbols in their work. A listing of these mythic gods and goddesses, observable in the folklore and ethnographic studies of many traditions, is given in the Appendix.

Specialist psychopomp spirits of traditional cultures, not surprisingly then, are found in accounts of shamanic practice today. In Korea, for example, the psychopomp, merging into the role of the Emissary Spirit from the World of Darkness, "sweeps the road" and then, taking on the role of the departed, "walks into the afterlife." The Bororo in Brazil have a special "shaman of the souls" who connects the departed soul with ancestor spirits who then conduct it safely through its dangerous journey in the land of the dead.

Some of these spirit allies for the psychopomp live on, too, in ordinary language. The German town of Berchtesgaden, for example, derives from the goddess Berchta, and the nation of Holland from the goddess Hulda. Such psychopomp allies are also found in films, books, comics, and other media of popular culture.

Modern shamans, then, have available "tailor-made" help for psychopomp work. Beginning practitioners can call on these "experienced professional" spirit allies to assist them in the process. For example, they can call on those spirits who derive specifically from the ethnicities or day-jobs of the discarnate souls, clients, or themselves, such as asking Morgan Le Fay to heal a soul with a Celtic background, or Odin to heal a soul with a military one. The only caveat is that today's shaman should call on such allies only after familiarization with the culture from which they came.

Thematics and Symbology

Practitioners can use the rich mythopoetic themes and symbols associated with these psychopomp spirits in many ways. The thematics are clear. Many of the spirits guard the passageway between earth and the afterlife, or have animals who do so, suggesting a primitive sort of "Peter at the Pearly Gates." The spirits seem to have a special compassion for certain groups, such as risk-taking adventurers like seafarers and warriors (the gods and goddesses even serve food to fallen fighters), children, victims of storms (like those who drowned or were struck by lightning), forgotten people, prisoners, and shamans. In contrast, they have little tolerance for ghosts who harass living humans, and go out of their way to provide an attitude adjustment.

Many of the traditions have a transition stage between earthly life and afterlife when the soul is "purified" from past issues so it can enjoy the beyond, free of psychospiritual malaise. Bureaucratic religions may refer to this realm as limbo, purgatory, bardo, or other term.

Both male and female spirits serve as guides, escorts, and guardians of souls. Women, though, clearly have the principal place, outnumbering men two to one in the listing. Postmortem care by female spirits, who manifest as bird-women or fish-women (mermaids), predominates. Female psychopomp spirits protect, rescue, and comfort discarnate souls but banish those who cause humans trouble. Male ones, in contrast, serve as ferrymen, patrollers, and judges of fitness for the afterlife.

The theme of moving water, in the form of rain, rivers, and seas, is common, as are associated symbols such as bridges. Journeys of psychopomps to contact souls in nonordinary reality often involved a passage across moving water in a boat, often with canine helpers. Among the South African Cape Nguni, for example, ancestor souls dwell in rivers. To Nigerian Igbo shamans, the physical and spiritual worlds are separated by water. The Dusun of Borneo picture the road of the dead as crossing a stream; Twana shamans, when looking for souls in the other world, cross a river; and Manacica shamans lead departed souls across a river by means of a bridge guarded by a god.

The "funerary bridge," not surprisingly then, is common in the psychopomp tradition. Iranian, Lolo, and Caucasian souls cross a bridge to the afterlife, while for the Telumni Yokuts, the Land of the Dead is separated from that of the living by a stream with a bridge guarded by a bird. In one story from Chinese folklore, the righteous soul goes to the afterlife by way of a bridge, whereas the unrighteous one must swim while being assaulted by demons. Among the Na-Khi, the deceased soul must cross a bridge blocked by demons, who are cleared by the shaman-psychopomp, who eventually leads it to the realm of the gods. Crossing some form of water is seen by peoples the world over as a means of moving from a dead old existence to a different living new one, as seen in Rose's role in the film *Titanic*. Not only does water purify, as in ritual ablutions, but it initiates one into a new life, as in baptism.

So, the symbols of boat and ferryman appear often in psychopomp practice even today. Some peoples like the Vikings disposed of their dead in a boat, while some ancient Greeks described death as a journey across water in a ship of death. Indonesian shamans use ships of the dead to transport the deceased to the beyond. In Borneo, souls of the dead are thought to travel to the spiritual realm by ship, and Dyak mourners of Borneo chant songs describing the deceased's journey to the afterlife by way of boat. Korean shamans use a paper boat moving across a long white cloth symbolizing a river, so as to enact the soul's crossing to the "other shore." Melanesian and Salish shamans use a spirit boat to journey to the Land of the Dead to help departed souls. Tungus shamans use a boat to travel to nonordinary reality, employing fish-spirits to lead it, while among Chukchee shamans the drum is seen as a canoe for traveling to the world beyond. The Vasyugan-Ostyak shaman uses a boat and shoulder-bone oar to cross to nonordinary reality. An ancient Egyptian belief held that the dead live in the Boat of the Sun. Among the Akan in Ghana, the soul must cross a river after paying the ferryman.

Certain therianthropes (part human and part animal, or human-animals, or wereanimals) are associated with psychopomp work. These likely hark back to shamans who "merged" with their animal helping spirits, namely were voluntarily "possessed" by them, and so took on their shape in whole or in part.

A few types of species predominate in the mythology. Not surprisingly, given the water motif, aquatic animals are evident, such as fish, sea snakes, and mermaids.

More common, though, are canines or werecanines like hounds, wolves, jackals, and dogs. For Koryak shamans, the passageway into nonordinary reality, for themselves and the deceased, is guarded by dogs. Inuit shamans are only able to pass by dogs guarding the entryway to the Other Side by showing no fear. Tungus shamans use wolves as helping spirits on psychopomp missions.

This should not be too strange to modern people. In esoteric lore even today, the dog family is well known for being especially sensitive to spirit entities, be they ghosts or human remote-viewers. In research today as well, dogs have been found to be impressively psychic, knowing for example when their owners are coming home. Canines also make great transporters (sled dogs), trackers (bloodhounds), guides (seeing-eye dogs), road companions (Charlie in Steinbeck's *Travels with Charlie*), protectors of the pack (guard dogs and K-9 units), loyal pals (man's best friends), rescuers (cadaver dogs), law enforcers (customs dogs), herders (border collies), and healers (therapy dogs)—all such functions being useful for, and so observable in, psychopomp work. In my own practice, canine power animals have proven particularly helpful, especially with child souls.

Birds are even more common, such as crows/ravens, swans, cranes, and vultures, or werebirds such as angels, appearing in nearly 1 out of 5 cases in the listing. Historically bird spirits have been used for many kinds of shamanic practice; the "ability to turn into a bird is the common property of all kinds of shamanism," observed Eliade, with feathers being "the magical sign of the mystical power to fly." Ancient Taoist practitioners were called "feather scholars." Ancient shamans in India needed wings to traverse the boundary between the worlds, while today Manchu ones use bird figurines to help on their journeys, and Siberian ones have pictures of birds on their costumes. Yakut shamans dance their journey by imitating a bird's flight and are accompanied by water birds. Yakut and Dolgun ones use stakes and trees with birds carved on their tops for journeys to nonordinary reality. Inuit shamans fly in this reality, spreading their arms like birds. Mongol shamans have wings on their shoulders and feel they are changed into birds; the Tungus shamaness flies into the air as soon as she acquires her magical plumage. Buryat shamans likewise are said to take the form of birds.

Bird spirits are especially helpful for shamans when dealing with death. "Birds," as Eliade put it, "are psychopomps." Not surprisingly, then, shamans adopt bird features for their psychopomp work. The Dyak shaman, when escorting deceased souls to the Other Side, takes the form of a bird. In China, the crane is viewed as helpful in escorting discarnate souls. Yokut shamans cross rivers full of obstacles, which are cleared by their bird helpers; Orochi ones use eagle helping spirits; Goldi ones ride a long-necked bird spirit back to earthly reality. During Altai funerals, bonesetters make bird sounds as they instruct the dead soul to go to the Other Side. Mongolians prefer that dead bodies be consumed by birds rather than by land animals, so that the winged creatures can easily and quickly fly the departed to the afterlife.

Ravens among the Kamchatka Koryak are conduits to the afterworld, carrying offerings of meat from this world to the ancestor spirits; women preparing the funeral caw like ravens as they work. Ravens and crows are also associated with death in many other cultures.

Birds symbolize the freedom brought by death, namely the shedding of the gravity-heavy physical body by souls so they can roam free, unencumbered. Some traditions, then, use the flying of birds as a symbol, not for spirit allies, but for the flights of departed souls themselves. In Eurasian shamanism, birds, wings, and feathers signified vehicles carrying the soul off to the world of the dead. Greek shamans provided deceased souls with wings to cross to the afterlife. Among Native-Americans, crows themselves may embody dead souls, and Sumatran shamans see such souls perched like birds in a tree. The Egyptian Book of the Dead depicts the deceased as a falcon flying away, while the Yakut say that the soul takes the form of a bird after death. Among Finno-Ugrians the souls of the dead were able to reach the afterlife by flying like birds or by crossing a sea, river, or lake in the form of an aquatic animal like a swan.

The notion continues to this day. Studies of afterlife communications by researchers Joseph Higgins and Chuck Bergman showed that modern people "have reported feathers floating down upon them, within a closed space, when the thought of a [deceased] loved one entered their minds." This phenomenon, they add, is often "witnessed by friends and family."

The joint appearance of canines and corvids—dogs together with birds—is especially interesting, as in the case of the mythic Norse god Odin. Some wildlife biologists, we might note here, report that wolves and crows/ravens have a symbiotic relationship. When the birds spot an animal carcass they can't open up to feed upon, they call for the wolves to come, who then tear the hide open, and all enjoy a fine meal. Both sets of animals, too, are known for their trickery, at times a necessary strategy used by psychopomps.

Today's psychopomps, then, can use this mythic symbology, for example a river replete with ferryboat and oars, on their imaginal map of nonordinary reality during their journeys. They can call upon a canine or bird spirit, or a spirit manifesting as a canine or bird, and merge with it in whole or in part. They can incorporate symbols like bridges, feathers, and wings on their altars, costumes, medicine bags, drums, rattles, websites, and office walls. They can use mermaid "siren serenades," crow "caws," and "swan songs" in their chants and other vocalizations during ceremonies and dramatizations. Movement towards the West, the symbolic direction of death in certain traditions, might also be employed.

To sum up, the mythic helping spirits of psychopomps past are still around and awaiting the call of the modern practitioner. Waiting as well are the discarnate souls having trouble leaving the earthly plane. Modern shamans, then, with a little help from their ancient spirit friends, can help these souls return to Source.

A little birdie. One day while I was sitting on my house deck, a sparrow flew to one of the posts holding up the overhanging roof and started flying around crazily and chirping frantically. This happened twice again during the week. Finally I checked where the post met the roof—nothing—but where it met the ground

David Kowalewski, PhD

I saw that carpenter ants had reduced half of it to a fine dust. Right away I phoned a carpenter who put in a new post. Now, when I hear a little birdie telling me something, I check it out the first time.

CHAPTER 6

Trip Planner

Tricksters. The corvid family, well known in mythology for being tricksters, even shapeshifters, keeps us humans on our toes. One day while I was sitting on my house deck practicing a shapeshift into a pine tree, suddenly a blue jay—a species of corvid— that was perched in a tree far away flew off and headed straight towards my head. As it got uncomfortably close, I panicked, whereupon it screeched, pulled up sharply, and landed behind me on the rain gutter of the house. Apparently it had seen not me but a pine tree. But the demon of doubt attacked and I said to myself, "Well, maybe." I resumed my practice. Then another blue jay flew off from the same tree and headed straight towards my head. As it got uncomfortably close, I panicked, whereupon it screeched, pulled up, and landed on the gutter. "Yes!" I patted myself on the back, "I've tricked the tricksters!"

Psychopomps need to be well prepared before venturing out into the strange and unpredictable world of the spirits. Since the work is a highly advanced shamanic skill, one first needs to take some formal training from qualified and experienced teachers on shamanic journeying and especially psychopomp work, to practice shamanism in daily life, and to read as much as possible on afterlife communication. In particular, one needs to know what the helping spirits are, how to retrieve and contact them, how to cultivate them, how to use them, and so on. Some training in the topography of nonordinary reality is also essential. All this is necessary to make psychopomping soul-trips safe and effective. That said, below I offer some personal lessons from my own experience that rarely appear in the literature and that may be of added help to beginners.

Instructional Journeys

Before engaging in any shamanic practice, many shamans take a few journeys to their helping spirits in nonordinary reality for specific advice on how best to do the work. Here's an example from my own preparatory journeys about psychopomp work, which I took in a classroom during a training session.

Instructional journey.

I started along a road that curved to the left, designated by an arrow sign off to the side, which I then followed. Eventually a wereape (half-human and half-ape) appeared who, I was told, was a very ancient shaman who had merged with his ape helping spirit.

He told me that the journey of the human individual and species was to move slowly to the Light, but to do so dancing, because otherwise we will stay stuck. He said that dancing was the most ancient psychopomp technique for helping earthbound souls, because it was effective —dancing is a lot more fun than being stuck.

Crafty Canine then suggested, "Let's practice that." So I played the shaman and Crafty Canine played the stuck soul.

I proposed to the "dead soul": "Let's dance up to the Other Side."

"No," said Crafty Canine, pointing to its corpse on the ground, "because I can already dance with my body right down there."

But I objected, "It's a lot more fun dancing without all that physical weight and limitation."

Then Morbid Corvid 1 whispered in my ear, "Take its front paws in yours and whirl with it up to the Other Side," which I did.

One minute later, as I walked out of the classroom onto a road, thinking of doing psychopomp work in the future, I saw a construction sign with an arrow pointing to the left, which I followed. As I did, a crow suddenly dived and flew right over my head. I could hear the whooshing of its wings just a few feet away.

Case Selection

Since there are undoubtedly thousands of earthbound souls languishing in nonordinary reality, which specific ones are the best candidates for escorting to the Other Side? How does the psychopomp choose?

Here are some general guidelines I've found helpful. I personally have a problem with psychopomping one's own loved ones. There is too much emotional baggage that can obscure clarity. I get best results when, while still being compassionate, I have some emotional distance.

David Kowalewski, PhD

I also do best when I avoid cases that entail "frontloading," namely knowing a lot of information about the case, which makes projection of one's own knowledge and personal agenda more likely. Instead, I get best results when I start as a blank slate and let the information just come to me. So, while it's good to select cases you know something about, too much information can be a liability.

Here are a few ways that other shamans and I have used to select cases

{} Ask your helping spirits to take you to the soul(s) most needing help.

{} With clear and strong intent, call to yourself any deceased souls who want help.

{} Think about the people who break your heart wide open.

This last way I've found especially helpful. It engenders compassion, which provides a powerful energetic engine, and a clear and intense focus, for successful escorting. Trapped souls, as well as demons, are suffering beings and need healing, not self-righteous judgmentalism. It is love that attracts the discarnate soul. Personally, I have had a lot of academic experience researching political violence, corruption, and repression cross-nationally, and as a result have special sympathy for victims of such ills, such as dissidents assassinated during military coups, unionists targeted by death squads, refugees fleeing military massacres, and writers tortured by dictatorships. So, in this book you will see a lot of cases resulting from such abuses.

Sometimes psychopomps become magnets for discarnate souls needing help, and so do not select their cases but their cases select them. The ghosts may show up during dreams, since both the soul's earthbound state, and the shaman's dream state, lie at the boundary between ordinary and nonordinary realities, thereby facilitating communication. This kind of dream has a number of features distinguishing it from other dreams.

{} **Death motif.** Since most dreams do not deal with death, the psychopomp ones stand out. In my experience the entire such dream is about the death situation and nothing else. That said, while I see the death scene—how the person dies—I do not see the death itself.

{} **Violence.** The death is usually a violent one, causing enough desperation and panic in the discarnate soul to go to great lengths to seek out a shaman for help.

{} **Unfamiliarity.** Such dreams usually involve a single person totally unknown to the dreamer, and the situation too is totally unfamiliar. The person and situation, in fact, are often totally incongruous with the ordinary reality life of the shaman. This feature of unfamiliarity suggests to the psychopomp that the dream is about that other person and not oneself.

{} **Memorability**. Such dreams are usually vivid and sometimes tangible, involving physical disruptions during sleep, with very clear and impressive details and so easily remembered.

{} **Realism.** Such dreams have a realistic feel to them, not a "dreamy" one. They are like a news report, not a fantasy movie.

{} **Nonengagement.** Although within such a dreamscape the psychopomps are physically close to the person, they are emotionally removed from the death scene and do not experience the "dream death" themselves. Being passive observers, they are *in* the dream but not *of* it, and so, while compassionate, do not feel any panic, pain, or suffering, however chaotic and gruesome the scene. The dream, then, is not a nightmare.

{} **Futility.** The psychopomp dreamers feel no ability to change the course of events, knowing that the person's death is inevitable. There is an air of morbid finality about the situation, so even though the dreamers may know exactly how to prevent the death, they know it's impossible to do so.

{} **Synchronous aftermath.** After the dream an eerie coincidence may occur. For example, a psychopomp may dream of recently departed earthbound souls and then the next morning, while thinking of them in their own closed-up home, feel a strong icy wind blow by.

Below is a personal example. I dreamt of a young woman being suffocated to death, so the next day I made a psychopomp journey.

Midwest murder scene 2012.

To a prison where I saw the soul of a young woman who said her husband, now incarcerated there, had strangled her to death because she "drove him to it" with constant nagging.

At this point Crafty Canine whispered in my ear, "With a thousand cuts."

She said she didn't want to cross over because she felt guilty and wanted to make it up to her husband.

I suggested that she first needed to forgive him for whatever made her take revenge on him with her nagging in the first place, and then to heal him somehow. I said the best way to do that was to fill him with healing light every time he felt hurt from someone's words.

She asked how she could do that.

I called in an extra helping spirit, a healing specialist, and when it arrived, I told the woman, "This spirit will come and heal your husband every time you call." We then agreed I would come and help her move on whenever she felt ready.

A more dramatic case occurred one night when I was awakened by a loud metallic crashing sound and my body suddenly felt it had slammed into a brick wall. I was mystified until I went into town the next afternoon and saw a cross with fresh flowers standing at an intersection indicating a recent fatal vehicle crash.

Preparing to Journey

Failing to prepare, as famous basketball coach John Wooden always told his players, is preparing to fail. Successful psychopomp work depends on good advance work.

Before journeying into nonordinary reality, psychopomps always need to be full of power, since the presence of the dead can be nearly overwhelming. They should be full of healthy energy and well rested, and should avoid journeying if in a distraught emotional state. To do the work while tired, sad, and depressed is not only inefficient, but will in fact add to the heaviness of the earthbound souls. Bringing negative feelings to a negative scene is hardly helpful. "Physician," it is said, "heal thyself."

When journeying to a site of mass death, psychopomps usually protect and sometimes disguise themselves to avoid being immediately overwhelmed by suffering souls

David Kowalewski, PhD

seeking help. Psychopomps can also be "jumped," namely possessed themselves by a disturbed soul, or slimed. Enlisting the mythic allies and tools described above, like canine effigies and bird songs, is a powerful safeguard.

What time of day to do psychopomp work? Some say that nighttime is best for dealing with discarnate souls, especially malevolent ones, since this is the time they come out because they want to hide from the light—and the Light.

All good shamanic teachers tell their students to do the work only with the protection of helping spirits. For psychopomp work in particular, I make use of those helping spirits with whom I've developed an especially close, personal, and trusting relationship. These aides are not just useful but are essential, since they can do things that the psychopomp is unable to do. I find it best to ask any of those helping spirits who want to journey with me to come forward, rather than to call for any particular one. In my experience, they always know who's best for which job. An exception is when I deliberately want mythic psychopomp allies like Berchta or Odin for a specific reason.

I've also found it helpful to journey with a helping spirit of the opposite sex, who can help resolve any Mars-Venus impasses that may arise with souls of the opposite sex. Such a helping spirit can often understand a discarnate soul of its own gender better than can the psychopomp. Shamans can't assume, that is, that if they are "Mars souls" they will always understand "Venus souls" and vice-versa. The following case shows how well it worked to have a Venus helping spirit rescue a Mars shaman out of an awkward situation.

Turkish genocide of Armenians 1915.

To a mass grave of 30 women who were lying face down and who wouldn't look up. "Why don't you look at us?" I asked.

"Because our bodies have been violated and we're ashamed."

I said, "So then you need to make them holy again, right?"

They paused, then said yes. But I had no clue how to do that and was even feeling a bit embarrassed at the thought, so I asked my female helping spirit for help.

Beautiful Warrior told them, "Sit up on your sacrums [a word from the Latin for sacred or holy]," she said, "and you'll heal the desecration [a word from the Latin for violating something sacred or holy]."

They did and started smiling. Then a big bright light came into our midst. I merged with Beautiful Warrior and we stood in the center of the light. The women came up, put their arms around us, and we all left for the Other Side.

Without her help I seriously doubt that I would have struck just that right gender note. (Nonordinary reality is replete with symbols, so the plays-on-words often get dense. Note in this case, for example, how the women were lying face-down and so hiding their faces as well as their genital areas. Note as well the nearness of the sacrum to that area, the site of their desecration.)

I've found it best to use helping spirits for whatever role they want to play. My personal ones are most often helpful as social ice-breakers; protectors; warriors; jokers and tricksters for relieving tension between the soul and me; trackers and retrievers of the discarnate souls or their living loved ones; and guides to the Light. Power animals are especially helpful for bonding with child souls. Here's how Crafty Canine once helped me as a tracker and guide.

Libyan revolution 2011.

To the front lines where the forces of Qaddafi and the opposition were clashing. We saw a 12 year-old boy standing by his body and that of his father next to a destroyed car. He realized I was an American and, since his family supported Qaddafi, was suspicious. So I said, "I'm not involved in this fight, I would just like to help you."

He agreed. He said he knew he was dead, then asked, "But where is my father?"

"He went to another place, a peaceful one, and you can join him," I answered.

He said, "I'd like that."

I told him he needed to follow Crafty Canine, "who has a great sense of smell," in order to track down his father's soul. Right away Crafty Canine walked over to the body of the boy's father, sniffed his clothes, got the scent, and started tracking.

"Hurry up," I told the boy, "he'll take you to your father." *He left, happy, for the Other Side.*

Prior to journeying, shamans can get into special bodily postures, which scholars have derived from ancient shamanic images and artifacts, and which have been used over the centuries to facilitate psychopomp journeys. In this way they can employ to good effect the accumulated power of the primitive.

Finally, I find it necessary to drop completely any preconceptions about what will happen. Shamans need to be open and ready for the unexpected—in fact should expect it because that's likely what they'll get. The unexpected, in fact, is a good sign of authenticity. For this reason, taking many journeys in a row in short time that have similar features may make the psychopomp a dull shaman, as will too much control and rigor and scrutiny—the decline effect again. Variety is the spice of shamanic life. So, the more exciting and adventuresome the journeys, the more rewarding for all concerned.

Finding Discarnate Souls

Upon entering nonordinary reality, helping spirits will normally take the shaman right to the discarnate clients needing help. Also, it is said, certain shamans emit a special light, a beacon, that draws earthbound souls to them, in which case it might be said that discarnate souls "call the shaman" instead of vice-versa.

I like to experiment with the special psychopomping techniques of various cultures. In the Slavic tradition, psychopomps envision bringing their head down to their heart, which they then re-form into a head. Then they stand with their back against a birch tree and bounce their torso back and forth until everything physical disappears and only the energy body remains. Its bright light then attracts the soul, whom they welcome literally with "open energy arms."

Some psychopomps bring a familiar, preferably shiny metallic, object of positive emotional significance to the soul. The same principle applies with respect to favorite food and drink, music, tobacco product, and so on. Survivors of the discarnate soul can help the psychopomp with this kind of information about attractants.

Some shamans see discarnate souls gathering in a "staging area" waiting to cross over. Some too say that the psychopomp only has to open up a portal to nonordinary reality and the souls will appear. Others say that "era cues theory" is effective, that is, the shaman "cues" the soul to appear by wearing the clothes, playing the music, carrying the artifacts, and so on that were prevalent during the "era" of the soul's death. This helps explain why historical re-enactments of events like Civil War battles in the U.S. South are said to "wake up" and attract ghosts. (How many re-enactors participate in such events to see ghosts? A lot, I'll bet!)

Spiritual ceremonies as well attract souls, for example smoking the sacred pipe for the Lakota, as do secular ones at symbolic places and times, for example birthday parties. Other shamans use traditional divinatory ways to find souls, such as crystal ball gazing, throwing the bones, and the like.

Meeting and Greeting

Meeting the soul with gentle courtesy and establishing rapport is of paramount importance. The psychopomp can create such energetic resonance right away by clearly discerning the main emotion that the soul is manifesting, such as sadness or guilt, and then tuning into it. The case below shows how tapping into a youngster's love of playing with toys was used effectively.

Montana house 2011.

To the yard of a 5 year-old boy who had died of some illness. He seemed oblivious to being dead and wanted some toys to play with. I said, "If you go with Crafty Canine he'll take you to a lot of toys." He seemed thrilled at the prospect and went off with Crafty Canine to the Other Side.

The first question to the soul might bc, "Are you OK?" or "Are you doing well?" or if the soul is in obvious distress, "What's wrong?" Effective shamans always ask and never assume.

From the beginning of the encounter, psychopomps need to know if the soul realizes it's dead. If not, they need to gently introduce that idea. In the Tibetan Bön tradition, many souls are said to be obsessed with the last image they had in their mind when they died. Following this tradition, the psychopomp can ask, "What's the last thing you remember?"

Shamans never assume the soul knows it's dead. In the death-denying culture of the West especially, a sudden death may well come as a total shock with attendant disbelief. Also, since the soul can see its body, it reasonably assumes it can get back inside. Many humans, too, view death as the end of awareness itself, so when after dying they realize they are in fact still aware, they may reasonably conclude that they have not died but are still alive.

The next important issue is, "What happened?" The soul's story has a wealth of clues about the motives for being earthbound and the avenues for healing.

Finally, the soul must be asked if it's ready to go to the Light. Paying attention to the particular needs of the soul, the shaman aims at finding out how crossing over might satisfy them in some way. Here they need to be patient and give it time to ponder.

During the journey, the psychopomp may be given names, places, dates, and so on, but I've found it's normally a bad idea to ask for them. In the field of the paranormal, notes Dean Radin, because of "analytical overlay" by the logical mind, naming is "almost always wrong." If alphanumerics are relevant, I've learned, they will be given, and only for very good specific reasons.

Dealing with Problems

Although shamans should never argue with a soul about crossing over, they can still persist in their attempt. Above all they need to trust their helping spirits. Here's an example of surrendering to the power and wisdom of these aides.

Soviet gulag 1950s.

To Siberia outside the barbed wire of a Stalinist prison camp, where an Old Bolshevik had tried to escape but had been shot. He didn't want to leave because he still wanted to fight against Stalin for betraying the Workers' Revolution.

I said, "That's all past and eventually Stalin was discredited, and besides, working people have you to thank for spearheading the struggle and making it much easier for them to live in dignity."

He seemed surprised and thanked me.

I pushed on, "You're probably an atheist and don't believe in an afterlife, but trust me, you're alive after dying and need to go to the Other Side."

"I still need to fight," he objected.

I countered, "You'll be much more powerful on the Other Side."

At that instant Crafty Canine howled, and the man said, "I don't know if I believe you, but I know that dogs never lie." Crafty Canine then took him to the Light.

Asking questions, as in this case, often works better than persuasion because it makes the soul accept responsibility for its stance. Some questions I've found useful include:

{} "Don't you want to be free so you can better help the people you love?" This engages the well-known "helper's high" and "mirror neuron" effects.

{} "Don't you want to be carefree, not attached to all these earthly worries?" Here the soul is offered stress-relief, always a welcome thing.

{} "The loved ones you left behind want you to move on; so do you really want them to keep worrying about you?" Love and responsibility are used here, two powerful motivators.

{} "Do you think you're really helping your survivors by interfering in their lives, preventing them from overcoming their problems themselves and so learning from them?" Love and responsibility again.

{} "Wouldn't you like to just surrender all your emotional turmoil to the Big Mystery who will handle it all for you?" This taps into the soul's deepest need, namely to fulfill its destiny by surrendering to the Higher Power whence it came.

{} "Don't you think that your death was for a good reason, and so now it's up to your survivors to deal with it?" This query, again, brings out the deep knowledge of destiny, namely the ultimate need to return to Source.

{} "Isn't there a deceased relative or friend you want to see?" If the answer is yes, the shaman can call the deceased relative or friend to come from the Other Side and accompany the soul. I've used this bribe often to great effect. Both love and the soul's curiosity about "Whatever happened to …?" are enlisted here. Also, the soul understandably may be more likely to trust a familiar loved one than a strange shaman.

Overall, a focus on healing the soul with compassion, offering "psychotherapy for the dead," as Michael Harner put it, usually yields results. In the following case, such healing was effected with a simple offer of hope.

Texas mental hospital, 1985.

We saw a middle-aged woman sitting alone hunched over and looking at the floor. She looked up at us, confused.

I said, "We're here to help if you'd like."

She looked back down, and at that moment one of my female helping spirits walked up and started stroking the woman's back from her neck down to her tailbone, whereupon the woman started crying. Then she looked up, less confused, so I asked, "What's the last thing you remember?"

"Nothing," she replied.

I said, "You're here in the afterlife now, so you don't have to suffer anymore."

At this point she realized she was dead and looked visibly relieved, whereupon Crafty Canine trotted up and lay down in front of her, and she started petting it.

"Did you have a dog when you were young?" I asked.

"Yes," she said and smiled.

I said, "My dog can take you to a beautiful place." She stood up, wobbly, and Crafty Canine led her to the Light.

The psychopomp may even be able to turn malevolent spirits around to help us humans.

At the same time, though, while being sensitive, the shaman can be, and may need to be, very direct and blunt—the realm of the dead has little tolerance for pretense—and in the long run the soul will realize the healing power of the truth. Tough love is the way to go. I've learned never to be shy about it—I just go for it.

Escorting

The ancient traditions have many colorful ways of escorting the soul to the Other Side.

{} Among the Lakota, an effigy of the deceased may be made out of a stick replete with painted face. Then the stick is stuck into the ground for a while, while a spirit bundle containing a lock of the deceased's hair and other personal objects is made. Then the stick is held up to the sun to release the soul and send it back to Creator.

{} In the Wiccan tradition, practitioners may make a circle of protection, then open a "door" so the soul can move to the Other Side, to the West to the Summerlands. In like manner, the ancient Egyptians referred to dying as "westing."

{} Huichol shamans in Mexico guide the souls to the sky above the desert in San Luis Potosí.

{} Lolo shamans in China, during the funeral, remove beams from the roof to create an opening for the soul to leave for the Other Side.

{} Some shamans place a farewell prayer, written on paper or cloth, on the forehead of the deceased's body as a "passport" permitting transit across the boundary between life and death. Likewise, in some European cultures, a coin was put into the mouth of the corpse so the deceased could pay the toll for the ferry to the Other Side.

In modern individualist cultures, it's usually assumed that the psychopomp escorts souls one-by-one. Yet in the old days, group transitions were common. Pomo shamans might direct a "spirit boat" to take many souls to the Other

Side. In some cultures, psychopomps riding a horse might gather them together for a group soul-trip. Some shamans in Indonesia do a collective psychopomping after the souls are honored by surviving relatives with food, music, and dance at a funerary ceremony. Tibetan shamans as well do a group ceremony, a community fire rite, to clear the locality when too many souls are around, a practice that continues till today. Indeed in the coming decades, when the hosts of ghosts from the population explosion start showing up everywhere, group psychopomping may be the only efficient way.

Escorting a whole group of souls is especially appropriate, and successful, when they are closely bound by a similar traumatic, emotional, familial, tribal, generational, or occupational connection. For example, dead soldiers in the same military unit have an especially strong bond, and so will refuse to "leave their buddies" behind to die on the battlefield. If the shaman can find the leader of the group right away and convince him or her to go to the Light, the others are likely to follow.

In fact, in my own journeys, I've escorted two or more souls at a time in no less than 30% of the cases. For example:

Haiti earthquake 2010.

To a collapsed schoolhouse where five children came up to us, enamored with Crafty Canine and his Magic Sled. I let them pet Crafty Canine, then put two on its back and the rest into the sled, and they played together for a while. Then I asked the dominant child to go to the Light and told the rest to play Follow the Leader, which they proceeded to do.

Some shamans ask the soul if it has any messages for survivors, which they relay only if a healing purpose is served. A departing soul, for its part, may volunteer to help psychopomps from the Other Side in their shamanic work.

Ethical Guidelines

Shamanism, like all professions, has standards. When practicing the craft in modern skeptical cultures, psychopomps should do their work in private and never for entertainment purposes. However, sympathetic observers, in particular other competent shamans who are knowledgeable about afterlife realities, may be very helpful and even necessary, especially when dealing with malevolent spirits. A shamanic axiom is that group work is more powerful than solo work.

Many shamans never de-haunt a place unless the owner gives permission. Some hotels, resort areas, and the like make their living from "friendly spirits," and so psychopomps may be accused of "stealing ghosts." Some owners may also derive comfort and solace from deceased family members still "hanging around." What the psychopomp can do, however, is to point out that clinging to the deceased only prolongs the crossing of the discarnates and the grieving of the survivors.

The dignity of the soul must always be respected. Above all, it should never be forcibly crossed over. Responsible shamans also respect the privacy, confidentiality, and anonymity of both the soul and its survivors.

Lazarus. During my first week of training in shamanic healing, one afternoon a group of volunteer patients from the surrounding town came into the classroom

to be treated by us students. One of the patients, who had Lyme disease, was in especially bad shape, unable to walk without a helper under each arm. His face was a ghastly and even ghostly gray, and I was sure his next step would be right into the grave. My shamanic partner for the healing exercise was a kindly nurse with a lot of experience and a heart as big as a house. The teacher assigned the Lyme disease patient to the two of us. "Terrific," I thought, "my first attempt as a shaman wannabe, without any experience at all, and they give me Lazarus for God's sake!" My partner listened to my complaint and said, "You can just follow me if you want, but you really just need to follow your heart." We did our ceremony for Lazarus, who then stumbled out, after which I asked her, "Do you think we did any good?" "Oh yes," she said, "I saw the spirochetes come out of his body and fly out the window." "The whats?" I asked. She said, "The disease—he'll be fine." Next morning I'm standing in the breakfast line and hear a booming laugh behind me. I turn around—it's Lazarus! His face is pink and glowing, and his body is bursting with energy. Then I saw him, without any helpers under his arms, jauntily walk up to the serving tables and load up a big tray with food, and then do it again. I'm an expert now on Lyme disease, and on Jesus the shaman.

CHAPTER 7

Strategies

Goldenrod 1. At a shamanic training session I met a psychic whose power rocked my soul. Upon parting she told me, "Make a goldenrod tincture to strengthen your spiritual core." I went home and did just that. I also set out to connect more deeply with the plant, bringing its flowers into my house for decoration and drying its leaves for winter tea. Soon I was closer to Goldenrod than anyone in town. When I would come home from a miserable day of faculty meetings and other bureaucratic hassles, I would sit down in the middle of my goldenrod patch and watch the setting sun splash its light off the radiant flowers. "No problem," I thought, "I'm surrounded by gold."

In my psychopomp journeys I've found a number of strategies very helpful, especially when dealing with tough cases.

David Kowalewski, PhD

Logic

I've been surprised how many times simple logic works to move a soul on. Since the soul is in nonordinary reality, namely the world of the magical symbol, why would logic even work? But I've realized that the soul is oriented and bound to the earth, the world of ordinary-reality logic, so why wouldn't it work? Also, the soul is often in shock and confusion, and so welcomes the clear vision of the logical mind. Psychopomps, for their part, even while traveling in nonordinary reality, do stay connected to the earthly world of ordinary reality, and so can easily use their logical tools. In short, both soul and psychopomp are operating in an "in between" state, an "inter-world" so to speak, right where ordinary reality and nonordinary reality, logic *and* magic, interface.

This means, of course, that the psychopomp has to be ready to dip into a two-section toolkit, one for logic and the other for magic. Logic, I've found, works its own form of "magic" most often when the souls do not know they are dead or refuse to admit it, which was the case in almost 3 out of 10 episodes (28%). In still other cases, cool reason can effectively overcome unproductive, irrational emotion, as seen below.

U.S. invasion of Iraq 2003.

To Baghdad to a former communications center that had been reduced to rubble, with seven officials crushed to death and trapped inside. Anticipating a hostile reaction against an American, I hid while Crafty Canine told them that an American had come who wants to take them to the Other Side. They said, "We don't need any American!"

Crafty Canine asked, "Then where are your Iraqi spiritual helpers? Do you want to wait forever? At least listen to him."

They reluctantly agreed, and so I stepped out and said, "I'm sorry what happened, and many Americans have not supported this war and I am one of them—would each of you want to be blamed personally for all the crimes of Saddam?" That convinced them, and we all joined hands and flew to the Light.

The Customer Is Always Right

I'm ever amazed at how many businesses violate the cardinal rule of sales—the customer is always right. In the psychopomp business, this means suspending one's own spiritual tenets and working with the soul from its own perspective. Most modern shamans, in fact, do respect the shamanic nuclei of the bureaucratic religions (like Bön in Buddhism and Sufism in Islam). Also, not only do psychopomps not have the time to instruct the soul in their own values and practices, but also the soul's own beliefs are the ones that most resonate and so are the ones most important for psychomps to engage.

The following case shows how respect for the soul's religious objects can move it to the Light.

Mexican drug war 2009.

To a Mexican city where I saw a young man covered in blood and lying face down in a street. He had been hit in the face during a shootout and looked grotesque. He knew he was dead but was afraid to go to the Other Side: "I've done horrible things in my life."

I said, "We've all done bad things—you're not so special!" He almost laughed at this backdoor humor, so I pressed on.

"You'll be forgiven—it's what you have in your heart right now that counts."

"I didn't really want to do all those things," he replied.

Then I got a flash vision of Our Lady of Guadalupe and asked him if he believed in her.

"Oh yes!" he said, and pulled out a medal of her image from under his shirt.

I said, "Turn around," and there she was. He ran up and kissed her feet. Then she lifted him up and walked him to the Light as he cried uncontrollably.

Today we live in a globalized world, where a tolerance for the beliefs of others is more needed than ever. This is why shamans would do well to get familiar with all the major psychospiritual traditions.

Hurricane Katrina 2005.

To New Orleans to an upstairs apartment on Bourbon Street where a middle-aged woman was kneeling on the floor looking emotionally devastated. "I was raped by looters," she said.

"Why are you still here?" I asked.

"I'm a Catholic, and I sinned by offering my body to them if they wouldn't rob me, so they had their way with me, but then robbed me anyway, then killed me. I'm sure God won't forgive me."

I then told her the story of Jesus telling the crowd that wanted to stone the adulteress: "Let them who are without sin cast the first stone." Then I pointed out that the hurricane had brought a crisis, which causes people to do crazy things they later regret. "God will understand," I said. She was joyful then and went to the Light, but before she went through she turned around and blew me a kiss.

Trickery

Some helping spirits are tricksters, who love to upset stuck-in-the-mud routines, and so can be useful to psychopomps for getting souls "unstuck" from the earthly plane. Some animal totems that have been used in psychopomp work—birds like Crow/Raven and canines like Coyote and Fox—are well-known tricksters in Native-American and other lore. So as well are Hermes in the Greek, Loki in the Norse, and Fairies in the Celtic, traditions.

Shamans, then, worldwide over the millennia, have used trickery as a ploy. But some of today's Western shamans, many of them raised in the Puritan tradition in some form or other, have ethical problems with this. Yet not a single one of my teachers—all of them highly ethical as far as I could tell—have ever frowned on it, and I've found that it arises spontaneously during journeys, feels right, does no harm, and relieves suffering. It works. Not using it, in turn, might mean a lost opportunity for freeing the stuck soul. Shamans and their helping spirits are pragmatists, not purists. In 6% of the episodes, such a strategy arose and proved useful.

Trickery is especially effective when the soul stubbornly resists crossing over, as the case below illustrates.

U.S. invasion of Vietnam 1968.

To a battlefield where the smell of smoke and the sound of exploding shells reminded me of the helicopter scene from Apocalypse Now. *I started shaking and buzzing, just like during my near-death experience, and right away a blonde, flat-topped, square-jawed American soldier came up and asked, "Where are my buddies?"*

I said they went to the Other Side and asked if he wanted to go too.

He said, "I have to find them."

I replied that they are waiting for him, but he was unconvinced. Then I said, "They're having a drinking party and are waiting for you."

"Then let's go!" he exclaimed.

Trickery also works well with children, whose world is far more fluid and magical than that of adults. For them, imagination often trumps logic as a reality test.

Indonesian genocide of East Timorese 1975.

To a shelled schoolhouse outside of Dili where three 7 year-olds were playing in a classroom. They said that when the military shells started exploding and the fires broke out, all the other children had run outside. The three were waiting for them to come back, because they were afraid that, since the schoolhouse had already been reduced to rubble, the area outside might be the next target. Clearly they didn't know they were dead.

I told them that Crafty Canine and Morbid Corvid 1 would protect them, so we went outside. I asked them if they were tired of their old games and wanted to play a new one.

They eagerly assented, so I said, "It's called Follow the Leader—just follow Beautiful Warrior wherever she goes." They did so, and she led them through the Light.

In this and the following case, it is clear that trickery may be necessary when the souls don't realize they are dead.

Pennsylvania boys orphanage 1912.

Beautiful Warrior told me to hover over the site so I could watch the death. I saw a group of boys next to a cliff. Two of them were arguing, and suddenly one pushed the other over the cliff, causing him to tumble, hit his head on a rock, and break his neck. The victim was floating over his body, so I asked why he was still there.

"I want to get even," he said, "but I can't get into my body."

I was at a loss as to what to do, so I turned to Beautiful Warrior. She asked the boy, "How old is that body?"

He said 11.

"And how old are you now?"

He looked confused and said he didn't know.

"Aren't you much older now?" she asked.

"I think maybe," he said.

She asked, "So, you don't really fit into that body anymore, right?" He nodded, whereupon she said, "Come with me and we'll see if we can get you a bigger body." She then led him to the Other Side.

Bribery

A closely related strategy is bribery, which works especially well with children, as every parent knows. I used bribery of some kind in 38% of the episodes, usually in the form of a promised reunion with a loved one or the offer of toys to children.

Haiti earthquake 2010.

To an apartment building that was now rubble where I found two children. Crafty Canine came forward, hitched to its Magic Sled full of toys. I gave a toy to each child. Crafty Canine then led me to a third youngster, a boy angry at dying so young. I gave him a baseball glove, which made him very happy. Then Crafty Canine led me to a young girl, to whom I gave a doll with a white face, but she wanted a black doll, so I ran my hand over the doll's face and made it black. Then Crafty Canine led me to a young man, whom I asked to tell the children a story, and then to a young woman, whom I asked to help the man care for the children. Then I told everyone to get into the sled, which Crafty Canine then pulled to the Light.

Some shamans bribe souls with a few shots of brandy. How's that for using "helping spirits" to lift someone's "spirit" into the "nonordinary reality" of the "spirit world"?

Reunions

When discarnate souls ask to be reunited with loved ones before agreeing to cross over, the psychopomp often must act like an overworked chairperson of a family or class reunion. Usually this happens at sites of mass deaths, especially accidental ones, where separation from loved ones is common. In such cases the psychopomp may have to tell the soul, for example, "Your deceased family members want you to join them—they are waiting for you at a family reunion 'at home' on the Other Side," a strategy that often works well.

The psychopomp brings about many kinds of reunions during journeys. The soul may want to join other earthbound souls, or crossed-over souls, or living survivors, or some combination of these. The desired reunion may involve family members, workmates, lovers, and even pets. In the case below, I reunited deceased family members.

Rwanda genocide 1994.

To a deceased woman next to a hut and her two deceased children playing far away. I asked her, "Why are you here?"

She said stubbornly, "I want to tell off my husband who fled into the forest and let us get killed."

I said, "That's not fair to the kids—let them go."

She agreed, and I took them to the Light, where I saw their grandmother—her mother—standing with a knowing look. When I came back, I told the woman, "I saw your mother and she wants you to come up too."

She didn't believe me, so I described her mother in full detail and then she knew it was true. Then I clinched it: "And your children want you too."

The appearance of a parent from the Other Side, as the above case suggests, is a powerful incentive for deceased offspring to go there too.

Especially during bloody political conflicts, the deceased often need to reunite somehow with their deceased or living comrades-in-arms before agreeing to leave.

Colombia revolution 2011.

To Bogatá where I saw a young politician who had been gunned down by a sicario *hitman. He said, "I know I'm dead, I expected it, and now I'm trying to help my comrades."*

I asked how that was going, and he said he wasn't having any success but that he couldn't leave them. I asked if he was working alone.

"Yes, I have no help."

I said, "If you let me take you to the Other Side, you can link up with your deceased comrades and maybe start being more effective—want to try?"

He agreed, and when we came to the Light, some of his comrades sprang out and they all had a happy reunion.

Battle

Ancient shamanic accounts of psychopomping and other journeys sometimes involve full-scale battles with dark forces. While such reports are undoubtedly overplayed by today's ethnographers for dramatic effect, sometimes shamans do in fact need to don their armor and wage war for their clients, literally becoming "ghost busters." Or, to put it more humbly, they go into battle together with their helping spirits who do the heavy lifting.

I've found that such battles, which occurred in 3% of the episodes, are likely when certain souls whose psychospiritual immunity has been compromised by trauma or some other cause have been abducted by nefarious spirits who refuse to release them (in the same 3%). In such cases, a spirit war ensues. As a psychopomp, I do not aim to hurt or defeat or destroy the abductors, but merely to defend the captured souls as well as myself for the sake of moving the souls on. Still, such cases can make for a wild ride, such that by the end of the following journey I was starting to feel like the Indiana Jones of the Dead Set.

Turkish genocide of Armenians 1915.

Just as I entered nonordinary reality, Crafty Canine told me that this case would be difficult and so I would need some backup. I put out an All Points Bulletin to my helping spirits, and soon Beautiful Warrior, Native-American, and two others showed up. We came upon three Armenian men lying face down in the mud, with three armed Turkish soldiers standing above them laughing. The Turks had sodomized the men, then returned to Turkey where they died, but then came back to the scene to repeat their nefarious deeds in nonordinary reality.

We told the soldiers to leave, but they refused. Crafty Canine then jumped forward and snarled, Beautiful Warrior dive-bombed them, Native-American shot arrows, and one of the special helping spirits whom I had called shot love rays, but still they refused to go. Finally another special helping spirit, my exceptional heavy-hitter ally, drove them off.

The three Armenians, though, did not want to leave since they felt ashamed and humiliated, unwilling to face their compatriots on the Other Side.

We told them, "This type of thing has happened to thousands—and much worse—so your compatriots will understand." This convinced them, so my helping spirits took them to a river and cleaned them up, fit them out with new clothes, and even gave them haircuts. Then they all left for the Light.

Note here the richly symbolic cleansing of the desecration and shame in the river. Think: moving water!

Purpose beyond Self

Quite naturally, traumatized discarnates are self-absorbed, trying to figure out what happened, how to reunite with loved ones, and so on. This self-absorption, however, binds them to the earthly realm. I discovered, then, that if I could convince them to shift their awareness to a wider mission beyond self, the bindings would fall off.

In the case below, I used a sense of professional loyalty to free the soul from its own reflection.

Mexican drug war 2011.

To Juarez where a young man was running frantically around a decapitated body in the middle of the street, crying, "They didn't have to do it!"

I calmed him down and found out he was a journalist who was sad at leaving behind a wife and two young daughters. I said that he could help his family from the Other Side, but he didn't seem impressed. But when I said he could also help living journalists report on the drug war, he started to get animated but then checked himself.

"I don't believe in the 'Other Side'."

I said, "I'll take you there. If there's nothing there, you'll lose nothing, but if there is, then you'll gain something."

He agreed, and when we came to the Light, out stepped three deceased Mexican journalists who greeted him with hugs.

In the next case, I called the soul to its "expanded self," giving it a purpose for the sake of redeeming its "failed" earthly life.

Montana house 2012.

To a middle-aged man very confused and sad who didn't know what to do. He felt his life had been a failure.

I saw that he was suffering, but also that he was very compassionate. I said, "You suffered, but became better and not bitter. If you go to the Other Side, you can use that compassion to help us struggling humans."

He came alive, as if suddenly everything made sense, and said he would go. I asked if he wanted an escort, whereupon he looked at Native-American: "Sure, I always liked Indians." So the two then left together.

After this soul-trip I realized that sufferings crack the heart wide open and can make it more compassionate, unless being bitter about those sufferings closes it up again. The man in this journey kept it open, and is now helping us deal with our sufferings.

Attitude of Gratitude

Fixation on one's own suffering binds discarnates to the earthly plane. But if the psychopomp can get them to shift perception towards the beauty they've experienced, then the heaviness dissolves and they almost float to the Light. As a Seneca medicine woman once told me, "Thankfulness is the cure for everything." She was not exaggerating.

Rwanda genocide 1994.

To the Congo River where I saw an old man, a Tutsi, lying face down right next to his body which was lying in the water. When I asked why he was there, he said, "I need to help my people."

I said, "But you're dead." He said he wasn't. I said, "Yes—watch," and lifted his energy body up high so he could see his physical body floating downstream with the current.

"I still want to live on earth," he said.

I replied, "It's over, and you've lived to a ripe old age—most Africans die much younger. Aren't you grateful?" He smiled and admitted he was. Then I pointed out that right now the Tutsi are a small minority and completely overpowered, and that most people around the world don't care enough to make a difference. "But you can still help your people," I said.

"How?" he asked.

"On the Other Side you'll find Tutsis you can work with to make your people safe."

He was surprised and asked, "On the Other Side there are a lot of Tutsis?"

"Of course," I answered.

"Then I'll go," he said.

It's gratifying to see how a little celebratory "pomp and circumstance" can lighten up a morbid scene.

Healing the Wounds

When you're sick in bed, you usually don't want to get up and leave. The same is true of soul-wounded discarnates. The psychopomp, then, often needs to heal the wounds of the soul before it's ready to move on.

In the case below we treated a woman deeply wounded by torture.

Cambodian Killing Fields 1970s.

To a small hut where a rich middle-aged woman, her face dark and distorted with hate, was staring down at the floor. She said the Khmer Rouge had tortured her to find out where she had hidden her jewelry and then killed her.

I asked, "Can you forgive?"

"No," she replied.

Crafty Canine then said, "Wait a minute," and flew off through the Light and came back with three poor Cambodians who had been her chauffeur, cook, and gardener. They began to remind her how she had mistreated them, hit them, and fired them for trivial reasons. She started crying, and they said, "We forgive you."

I jumped in and asked her, "So can you forgive the Khmer Rouge now?"

She said yes eagerly. I was surprised how easily she had switched, and asked why. She said she realized that the Khmer Rouge had modeled their ruthless behavior on the old elites. "So in a way," she said, "I was responsible for my own torture and murder." Her face was glowing with light when she crossed over.

Data Bits

Sometimes psychopomp work is as simple as providing a little bit of information. The following case shows how shamanic data-retrieval can be used towards a good end.

El Salvador revolution 1980s.

To the San Salvador body dump site where I saw a male university student who had been tortured and killed. I asked, "Why are you still here?"

"I haven't done enough, I've failed."

I said, "But now the Salvadoran president is from the FMLN—you won!" He didn't believe me, but then I showed him a newspaper and he was overjoyed. I said, "You gave your life for a noble cause, which is the best thing a soul can do, so you can go to the Light completely at peace." He did just that.

Flattery Will Get You Everywhere

As the case above shows, low self-esteem can keep souls from moving on. But with just a little praise, they can be lifted up and crossed over.

Yemen revolution 2011.

To the outskirts of Sanaa to a crumpled car, next to which was a man kneeling over his body. Beautiful Warrior told me he'd been killed in Sanaa but the army had put his body in the car, driven out to the desert, and crashed the vehicle to make the death look like an accident.

The man told us, "I was too young to die."

Beautiful Warrior, who now appeared as a young Muslim woman in a headscarf, said, "But you fought and died for a noble cause," and he cheered up right away.

But he said, "My people still need freedom."

At that point Morbid Corvid 1 flew in and said, "You can't do anything more here, but we can take you to where you can do some good." He agreed and left to the Light.

Archetypal Resonance

Note in the above case how Beautiful Warrior activated the energy of the Warrior archetype to reanimate the moribund soul and lift it out of its funk. Shamans work in the realm of energies, and none are more important than the classical archetypes, such as Scribe, Sidekick, Queen, and so on. Below are two more examples showing how the powerful energy of an archetype can propel the soul into the Light. In the first, the soul is reminded of its Martyr energetics.

Syrian revolution 2011.

To a small town where a young man was looking for his fellow fighters. He was confused, so I said, "They've left but they're still alive."

At this he looked shocked, realizing he might be dead. "If I'm dead," he said, "then where's my body?" I sent Morbid Corvid 2 to look around, and soon it returned and took us all to see his body lying behind a building a short distance away.

I said, "You've become a martyr for freedom," and he looked happy. I said, "Want to join the other martyrs?" He *looked even happier. Morbid Corvid 2 flew off and I told the man to follow. It went through the Light and brought back three fellow fighters who hugged the man and led him back through to the Other Side.*

In the next case I shapeshifted sorrow into pride by comforting the disturbed soul with its Hero archetype.

Egyptian revolution 2011.

Upon starting this journey, my helping spirits told me to make my energy body vibrate just like the buzzing I felt during my near-death experience so I could become a powerful soul-magnet. I did so, and right away upon descending into Cairo a student rushed up—confused. He said he didn't know what had happened, so I asked about the last thing he remembered.

He said he was at a demonstration when he leaned over to pick something up and felt a blow to the back of his head.

I asked, "Do you remember getting up?" at which he shook his head, so then I said, "You died a hero for your people—you should be proud."

He said he wanted to stay with the protesters, but I said they in fact were winning the struggle. He said he was also worried about his girlfriend.

At that point Crafty Canine went into hound dog mode and started sniffing around. We followed and soon found her still alive, but she was crying about her dead boyfriend. So I told Crafty Canine to tell her that he is OK and wants her to have a happy life without him. After witnessing this, the man finally looked happy and went to the Light.

Note here how the vibrating of my energy body just like it had "buzzed" during my near-death experience was like tuning a radio to a desired channel, which immediately picked up the resonant ghostly "signal" nearby.

Negotiating

The psychopomp sometimes needs to be a flexible negotiator. The case below reveals the shaman as deal-maker.

Montana town 2008.

To a middle-aged Native-American man who was kneeling and crying. He told me, "My son died and I'm a medicine man but couldn't bring him back to life."

I asked, "How did he die?"

He said his son was riding a horse down a hill when he fell and broke his neck and back.

"You're dead now just like him, so will you let me take you to the Other Side?" I asked.

"No," he said, "I need to see my son's spirit." I didn't know if, because of the sudden violent death, his son was earthbound or if he had already crossed over, so I couldn't promise the father that his son would be on the Other Side.

"If I bring your son, will you cross over?" I asked, and he said yes.

So I asked Crafty Canine what to do, and he said, "Let's go to the accident site and see." So I rode it there and saw the son above his body and told him that his father had also died and wanted to see him. He looked very happy. So the two of us rode Crafty Canine back, and father and son went to the Light together.

Morbid Humor

Although psychopomping is deadly serious, it doesn't have to be humorless. Michael Harner tells the story of a scholar who was leaving a group of shamans he had been researching for months in their native communities. "Thank you so much," the scholar said, "but did I miss anything?" The shamans fidgeted and looked at their feet, not wanting to embarrass him. "No, really, it's OK, you can tell me," he insisted. They finally looked up and said, "You missed ... the ... humor!"

Earthbound souls have a distinctly heavy energy, so anything that can lighten them up, even if it's a bad joke, is helpful. This strategy is not sacrilegious, just incongruous—in the best tradition of the best humor. I'm a big fan of what I call "sacred absurdity"—sacred because the humor helps us withstand horrible pain and suffering. One can use this kind of "morbid levity" with deceased souls, then, to good effect, and have fun in the process, just like the ancient shamans. Just because you're dead, quipped famous researcher Elisabeth Kübler-Ross, doesn't mean you can't laugh.

Yet, think about it: Try cheering someone up who just died—not an easy job. But it *can* be done. Watch.

Hurricane Katrina 2005.

To New Orleans to the roof of a flooded house, but no souls were around. Crafty Canine then led me to a flooded street with a boat carrying a middle-aged man's bloody body inside. But still I saw no soul. Then I realized that the house we had first landed on was his, so we returned and went inside and saw him sitting in a big chair looking very depressed.

David Kowalewski, PhD

He said he had been killed by looters because he wouldn't give them the supplies in his boat. He wasn't sure if he wanted to cross over.

I realized he was traumatized, so I pointed to all the devastation and said, "Hey, what could be worse than this?" He laughed at the morbid humor, which I realized was very similar to what I had once heard a blues singer say: "When I sing the Blues, I'm so sad I'm happy!" So I asked him if he would join me in singing Sometimes I Feel like a Motherless Child. *He agreed and we left for the Light, jamming happily.*

Yes, laughter *is* the best medicine, in this life *and* the next. That's why I like to call shamanism The Laughing Way. When I told a fellow shamanic practitioner that I was doing a lot of psychopomp work, she replied, "Oh, so you're stuck in a dead-end job." Shamanism doesn't pay well, except for the laughs.

Goldenrod 2. The fall semester was just underway. Meeting after meeting and other bureaucratic hassles had given me the urge to jog my cares away around my property. As I passed by my small patch of goldenrod, I thought I saw a flash of light, but when I stopped and looked I saw nothing. On the next lap, I saw another flash, but this time more clearly—a column of yellow light surging towards the sky. I stopped and waited—then saw another column, and another. I was mystified, but then "got the memo": The goldenrods were dying, their souls shooting up to the heavens as *golden rods* of light. I realized then that death need not be a tragedy but could in fact be a glorious event;

little had I known how beautiful a death could be. I imagined humans once dying like this—naturally and luminously—before they bought into civilization with all its neuroses and psychoses.

CHAPTER 8

Patterns

The Crying Way. I was sitting in a shamanic training session, listening to students describe their journeys to nonordinary reality. One student, an elderly woman, started sobbing uncontrollably in the middle of her account. When she was done the teacher said, "You know, shamanism is sometimes called 'The Crying Way'." After that training, during the following semester at my university, students would come into my office and suddenly break into tears for no reason at all. I started keeping a box of tissues on my desk.

As psychopomps gain experience, they start detecting common features in their work. Below I describe the most prevalent patterns I've seen in my journeys.

Emotional Bonds

The world of the dead is very alive with a variety of feelings that may keep souls earthbound. Yet a small handful keeps recurring.

Unfairness of "premature" death

When encountering teenage and young adult souls, one of the most commonly seen emotions is a sense of injustice at not having been able to live a long life.

Syrian revolution 2011.

To a young man crying next to his body which was lying in the street. He had been dragged out of his home by soldiers and shot. He said, "It isn't fair, I wasn't involved! I'm too young to be dead!"

When I asked if I could take him to the Other Side, he refused because of the circumstances of his death: "I can't make any sense of it!"

I responded, "Sometimes things don't make sense until later."

"Then I'll stay here until they do," he shot back.

Getting nowhere, I left Crafty Canine with him, and went to another body, that of a woman, next to which was the deceased soul who said she couldn't find her daughter. I told the woman to come with Beautiful Warrior and me, and Beautiful Warrior led us to the house of her living mother, where the deceased woman saw that her daughter was still alive and being cared for. I added, "I have powerful spirit friends who will also look after your daughter." She seemed to believe me and went to the Other Side.

Then I returned to Crafty Canine who was lying protectively next to the young man, who seemed to be in a better mood. I said, "If you let us take you to the Other Side, you'll probably be able to find out why you died so young." He said he'd give it a try and left for the Light.

Note the useful services provided by my helping spirits: Beautiful Warrior as scout and Crafty Canine as man's best friend. In the next account, my helping spirits simply shocked an aggrieved soul out of its sense of unfairness.

Mexican drug war 2011.

To Juarez where I saw a young man fixated on his mutilated body. "I don't deserve this!" he kept repeating, his head downcast. He told me, "My gang boss thought I betrayed him—I don't deserve this!"

When I asked if he knew he had passed away, he started crying. I said, "I can take you to a better place."

But he objected, "I can't leave my girlfriend, she's pregnant." At this point Crafty Canine and MC 1 appeared behind me, 3-times my size, and the man's eyes widened and his jaw dropped.

I said, "I have powerful friends. If you go to the better place, you may be able to help your girlfriend and child from there." He agreed and was led to the Light by my helping spirits.

Attachment to the good old life

Some discarnate souls who had lived a luxurious life find themselves befuddled and nostalgic at its loss. A useful tactic here is to stress the pleasure at letting go of the heavy burden of material goods.

Montana hospital 2008.

To a woman who had died of cancer and was holding on tightly to her bed. I asked why she was doing this and she said she missed her old life. I said, "You look exhausted."

She said, "I am." I asked why, and she looked confused and stumped.

"Could it be because you're dragging your old life behind you like a huge tractor-trailer without wheels?"

She acknowledged the possibility.

I said, "Let's try this. Just let go of half of your past life and see how it feels." She did and felt better. I said, "You look a lot better," and as she let go of the other half, she started floating up from the bed. I said, "How's that?" but she said she felt woozy. I called Crafty Canine and told her to ride it to the Light.

Detachment, for good reason, is a key tenet of the major spiritual traditions. Wallowing in the mausoleum of our past and shaking our fists at the gods are not good for you and me. "Let go and let God" is wise advice.

Despair

Due to the unrelenting pressure since the Enlightenment to be "optimistic" about "progress," seen especially in the "American Dream" that demands that everyone at least *look* upbeat, despair has been relegated to the dustbin of philosophy. Yet it is far more common than realized, unfortunately misdiagnosed as "depression" and pharmacologized as such, thereby being trivialized as a "mood" disorder rather than an existential one. Despair stays with us after death and, when fortified by skepticism, cynicism, agnosticism, and atheism, presents the psychopomp with a major challenge.

Afghan war 2011.

To Kabul where an American had been killed by a suicide attack. He first said he didn't know if he was dead, but then upon seeing my face said, "I guess I am—we all have to go sometime."

When I asked if he wanted to move on, he became bitter, cynical, and arrogant: "Why? This place is as good as any."

I asked if he wanted a drink, and he agreed, so we went to a secret bar, sat down, and right away he made a pass at Beautiful Warrior. I objected strongly, "Hands off! She's mine!" This got his respect, and he backed off. I told him how he had died, and that I could take him to a better place."

He was unsure, so I said, "I'll bring you back if you don't like it," and he consented.

From my journeys I've extracted some arguments about the value of suffering that have effectively lifted despairing souls out of their deep funk.

{} We suffer because we expect not to experience hardships, but later learn that life is just what it is: joy *and* sadness.

{} We have the power to choose to be bitter or better from suffering, to become more miserable or more compassionate—it's our call.

{} We learn that life can be so miserable that there has to be a better place—the Other Side.

{} Ordinary reality is only dismal when we humans lose our way and make it such.

But there are more dramatic and simple ways. One can show the soul the power of the spiritual realm compared to that of the earthly one.

Israeli invasion of Gaza 2014.

To Gaza City where an elderly woman was sitting in the street, slumped over, heavy with grief and despair. I asked, "Can I help?"

But she replied bitterly, "Nobody helps us Palestinians!"

I objected, then said, "Watch this." Morbid Corvid 1 grew to an enormous size and started flapping its wings, lifting her off the street. I said, "Your earthly life was heavy with grief, but your next life can be light with joy—see? Spirit is much more powerful than flesh."

Her eyes widened with light, so Morbid Corvid 1 was able to fly her to the Other Side.

The psychopomp can also turn the soul from seeing ugliness to seeing beauty.

Liberian Ebola epidemic 2014.

To a Monrovian clinic where four patients had been quickly buried. I asked if I could help them but they were bitter.

"You Americans couldn't help us when we were alive," they said, "so how can you help us when we're dead?!"

I was at a loss and turned it over to Crafty Canine. It led the eldest man to the edge of a cliff overlooking the ocean. "What do you see?"

The man said, "Something really beautiful."

Crafty Canine asked, "Isn't that what our souls are meant to be about, experiencing beauty?"

The man seemed to agree, so Crafty Canine said, "If you see only American or Liberian, rich or poor, white or black, you can miss the beauty, right? Turn around."

As the man turned, his eyes widened as I morphed into a radiant golden energy form. I realized he wanted to hug me, but he was thinking that his energy body was like his physical one, contagious with the virus. So I walked up and gave him a hug, after which the three other patients came up and we all had a long group hug. Morbid Corvid 1 then flew them to the Light.

The Navajo spiritual tradition is called The Beauty Way. They know something.

Addiction

Attachment to addictive substances of all kinds, like attachment to material goods, keeps souls earthbound. Addiction, as seen in the case below, is often comorbid with despair.

Montana town 2006.

To a car crash scene where a deceased woman started crying when she saw us. I was about to ask her to stop when Beautiful Warrior sat down and put an arm around her until she finally did stop a few minutes later. She said she had been driving drunk one night and gotten into a head-on collision.

"I got angry at the slow driver in front of me and tried to pass. I knew it was dangerous but I really didn't care if I lived or died."

I asked why and she said, "I was divorced three years ago because of my drinking, but instead of cleaning up my life I just drank more."

Then I asked why she drank, and she replied, "I'm miserable and don't see any joy around. Alcohol is the only joy I get."

I asked why again, but she was stumped. So I asked if she wanted to go to the Other Side, but she said, "No, I'm looking for another drink."

I saw that her eyes were all cloudy and black, so I asked, "Tell me exactly what you see."

She said, "Just darkness." I told her to turn around and tell me what she saw. She did and saw "Light" and her face started glowing.

"It's all a matter of what you choose to see," I said. She nodded, turned, and entered the Light.

Notice how Beautiful Warrior first provided the more indirect and patient "Venus nurturance" principle to balance my more direct and impatient "Mars git 'er done" one, and so softened the situation. I realized here that the female principle is a circle and the male one is a line, and when they work together they form a Medicine Wheel. Notice too how paying attention to the soul's energy body gave useful diagnostic information and so pointed to a resolution.

Shame

I found shame to be surprisingly common, but often for totally unexpected reasons.

European genocide of Native-Americans 1890s.

To an Indian camp in the Northern Rockies where two young braves were looking at the ground, ashamed because they had been killed by rampaging young white men with rifles, while they had had only bows and arrows.

I asked them if they wanted to cross over, but they replied angrily, "Who are you to help us?" Crafty Canine got very protective of me and bared his teeth, then howled and morphed into me. "We" then jumped on them and licked their faces.

This lightened them up, so I pressed on. "You know, some of us Palefaces greatly respect your ways—don't resent us, because we can help bring back those ways."

They said, "No, we lost the war, so Palefaces will never adopt our ways."

David Kowalewski, PhD

I was about to object, when Native-American came up, pointed to me, and said, "He's just as Indian as you are!" and told me to crank out a bow-drill fire, which I did. They were amazed. I said, "If you cross over, you can become even more powerful and help my people help your people, like Native-American here did with me."

Suddenly a light appeared with Indian spirit voices behind it, and soon the voices became a cold white wind blowing away the red-hot shame from the faces of the young braves, who then turned white themselves.

Behind the light we heard the Indian spirits laughing and shouting, "Those Indians just became Palefaces!" The braves then laughed too and left for the Other Side.

The protectiveness of my helping spirits, the color symbols, the energy body changes, and the morbid humor make this case one of my favorites.

Guilt

Remorse over one's past, especially the conditions leading up to one's death, often bind the soul.

Illinois traffic accident 2014.

To a car crash scene where we found a young woman who didn't want to cross over. She said, "I was responsible for the accident because I was texting and lost control and that's why the people in the other car died. I don't think I can be forgiven."

I asked her if she had ever heard of near-death experiences and she said yes. I said, "I had one of those and met the Light, and I can guarantee you that it's all-forgiving." I added that she was already halfway there because she had admitted her wrongdoing.

She looked relieved and walked through the Light.

Using one's own experiences with death not only gives souls useful information, but lends an authenticity that can convince them to move on.

Revenge

"If you seek revenge," goes a Chinese proverb, "dig two graves." Yet revenge is still common simply because, before *and* after death, it's so easy to justify, despite its ultimate lose-lose outcome. One of the typical emotional ropes tying down souls, then, is the failure to forgive. Either the soul cannot forgive those who hurt it, or those it hurt are unable to forgive it, or both. Not all is wine and roses in the spirit world. So, while in some way revenge may seem sweet to the avenger, it is toxic to the shaman's task. The psychopomp, then, may need to adopt a variety of measures to get all the parties involved to heal their wounds.

Miami drive-by shooting 2009.

To a parking lot outside a bar where a bloody body of a young man lay on the pavement. "What happened?" I asked.

He said, "I was just coming out of the bar when a car raced by and I heard shooting—someone was trying to kill the gang members who were milling around where I was standing. The gang members saw that I was hit but ran away, leaving me to die."

"Is that why you're still here?" I asked.

"Yes" he said, "they're going to pay."

I asked, "What have you done to them so far?"

"Nothing yet, I'm too weak to affect their world."

"Wouldn't you rather live in the light than the dark?"

He said, "Right now I want payback—they deserve it."

I told him, "The road to hell is paved with the word deserve—it really means to de-serve yourself." He was unmoved and even annoyed—logic wasn't working.

Then Morbid Corvid 2 stepped in front of him and said, "You can kill me, then you can get rid of the revenge—I'll take the hit."

The man seemed embarrassed at this self-sacrificing offer, at which point Crafty Canine walked up and asked, "Wouldn't you rather live in joy than in hate?" The man stood in stubborn silence, but I could tell he was weakening. At that point Crafty Canine jumped up on him and started licking his face and he started laughing. Crafty Canine kept it up until the man couldn't take it any more and ran into the Light, with Crafty Canine right behind him nipping at his heels.

From this case I learned not to engage the soul's destructive emotions, but to shapeshift them into constructive ones. I also learned not to depend on logic—powerful destructive emotions can easily trump it. In such cases, the shaman needs to deploy more powerful constructive emotions— from *power* animal helping spirits—like self-sacrificing love and joy, to overcome the destructive ones. Power animals, you've just seen, are effective precisely because they like going beyond the logical, the self-serving, and the calculating—namely they like doing things totally beyond the ken of the ordinary human way. The world of the dead is, after all, *nonordinary* reality.

Darfur war 2003.

To a burning hut where a deceased old man was sitting next to his body and those of his two deceased grandchildren.

He said he wasn't going to leave because he wanted revenge against the Janjaweed for the killings. But I pointed to the children and said, "How is that going to help them?"

"Eventually we'll win," he said.

"But the children are dead," I said, "and they can't fight—they're not big enough. They need to go to a better place. You shouldn't prevent this, because it's wrong!"

He said, "Then you take them." I said, "That's your job, you're their caretaker. Then you can come back." He agreed and left for the Light.

Tough love worked in this case—a useful lesson for the future. Also, again, I discovered that playing on other emotions like family responsibility and a sense of duty can overcome revenge, by showing the soul its true immediate mission vs. a self-indulgent distant agenda. When he realized this, his dark haze of revenge disappeared.

Spirits, Spirits, Everywhere

Besides the psychopomp's own familiar helping spirits used in a journey—the usual initial "call-ins"—other, unfamiliar, spirits often show up later to assist, invited or uninvited—the "walk-ins". This was probably the biggest surprise I found in my practice, even though my teachers, unanimously, had stressed that shamanism is all about teamwork. The greater the number of compassionate spirits around, the more powerful the process. Some of my journeys, in fact, got downright crowded, as other spirits arrived, invited (8%) or uninvited (25%), for a total of 1 out of 3 episodes. The stuck souls, in turn, responded very positively to the visitations.

Living shamans

The literature on shamanism has been almost mute about the fact that living shamans show up to help other living shamans in their work. More often, accounts tell of wars between shamans, which undoubtedly stems from the influence of mass media's infatuation with violence: "If it bleeds, it leads." Far more common in my experience, however, has been the generous, even touching, aid and comfort afforded me by powerful living colleagues in the craft.

Nicaraguan revolution 1980.

To a town where a massacre of Sandinista supporters by the U.S. government's contra death squads had taken place near a coffee plantation. I saw a female student crying and saying, "I'm still going to fight for my country."

When I said she needed to move on, she replied, "I'm not listening to any American—I can't forgive you."

I said, "Wait," and Beautiful Warrior came up to me and whispered that we should leave and get a Nicaraguan shaman. So Beautiful Warrior and I flew off to Managua to a basement apartment and saw a middle-aged man who came back with us.

"You need to leave now," he told the student.

But she said, "We need to win this war."

I interjected, "Yes, you've lost a lot of battles, but in fact you've already won the war!" She looked shocked, at which point the Nicaraguan shaman jumped in and told her the same. Then out of nowhere Crafty Canine jumped in front of her and she fell back in surprise.

"See," the shaman said, "this American has spiritual power."

She conceded and said to me, "OK, you can take me from here."

But I said, "No, that's your own shaman's job because, thanks to you, your country is not a banana republic anymore!" They both laughed and left to the Light.

Deceased shamans

One of the greatest joys of shamanism is working with the practitioners of the past. Deceased Inuit shamans, for example, keep working in the afterlife for the living. With a little help from my shaman friends of yesteryear, then, using good old-fashioned teamwork, I was able to resolve the following cases

Guatemalan genocide 1980s.

To the Mayan Highlands where I saw three infants lying on the ground. I took them up to the Light and, as I approached, a pair of hands reached through from the Other Side and took them from my arms.

Upon return a deceased Guatemalan shaman showed up and pointed to a young woman sitting with hate in her eyes. He asked me, "Can you help? I've tried everything."

The woman told me she'd been raped and was staying there because "I want him to pay just like I paid."

I didn't know what to say, so I asked Morbid Corvid 1 for help and it said, "Just ask her why she wants revenge." She said she didn't know. Again I asked Morbid Corvid 1 for help and it said to ask her what would make her feel better. I did but she fell silent.

I asked, "Will the world be better off if he suffers too?"

She started to cry and I held her. I realized then that revenge is caused by unresolved grief at our own suffering. She then said she was ready to cross over.

In the next journey, not only did deceased shamans help out, but so too did their helping spirits.

Haiti earthquake 2010.

To a collapsed apartment building in Port au Prince where two clusters of souls floated above the rubble—a group of five Vodou practitioners and a group of seven other Haitians. I went up to the practitioners, who looked hopelessly traumatized by the magnitude of the devastation. I said that their people needed them with all their helping spirits desperately right now.

They seemed to get animated from this moral support and right away called their helping spirits, who went through the building gathering up souls. Then their helping spirits and I psychopomped the first group of souls I had encountered, as well as the group they had gathered, to the Light. Then the practitioners told me they were going to stay behind to help their people.

The following case left me much impressed, showing me how much I still had to learn from the shrewd shamans of the past.

Typhoon Haiyan 2013.

Upon arriving in Tacloban in the Philippines, a deceased Filipino shaman who had once come to me in a dream showed up and said, "Don't look for dead souls, just hover above the city, emit your light, and they'll come.

I did so and right away a teenage boy came crawling over the rubble to me and said, "Help!" He begrudgingly admitted he was dead, but said he was waiting for his girlfriend.

I asked if she had died too but he didn't know. I was at a loss as to what to do, so I asked the Filipino shaman for help.

He said to the young man, "If she's dead, she's waiting for you on the Other Side, and if she's alive, she'll join you there when she dies."

The young man was skeptical, "How can that happen?"

The shaman said, "Love is a bond so strong that it survives death, because it's spiritual and not just physical." This convinced him, so he left for the Other Side.

One's own backup spirits

Most shamans have several helping spirits, but like me use only one or a few for any specific task. On some journeys, though, other helping spirits are useful for "beyond the call of duty" service to help the shaman out of a jam.

Hurricane Katrina 2005.

To New Orleans where I found a 6 year-old girl who had drowned in the street when a levy broke. She was crying and I said that her dad and mom, who were still alive, had told her to go to the Light and wait for them to come later and get her. She looked happy and left.

Then I called out to two other helping spirits of mine, who are experts at communicating with living souls, and asked them to tell her parents that their daughter was well and waiting for them on the Other Side.

Note here how the shaman helps to heal both the dead *and* the living.

Local spirit allies of the psychopomp's own spirits

One of my biggest surprises came when one of my helping spirits invited along one of its cousins who proved invaluable. In this case I realized that when the shaman is operating in a strange culture, the local flora and fauna totem spirits, who have a special familiarity and experience with that culture and the immediate situation, can be of great help.

Somali famine 2011.

I thought I was journeying with Morbid Corvid 1 alone, but when I looked back I saw that it had brought along a relative, Pied Crow, indigenous to East Africa. We landed at a roadside in south Somalia, where we saw a mother with her child, both dead, looking at the ground and feeling terrible. They knew they were dead but didn't think there was any better place, so were totally depressed.

Pied Crow then started tickling the mother under her arm until it got her to laugh. The child then took an interest in Pied Crow, whereupon it squawked and the mother and child both laughed. I told the mother I could take her to a better place where she could laugh and not be hungry all the time.

She said she had been a Muslim but didn't believe in Allah any more. "How could Allah let this famine happen?" she asked.

I said, "If Allah exists and is kind, he'll be kind to you because you took care of your child to the very end. What do you have to lose?"

She agreed that it was worth a try and Pied Crow then took them to the Light.

Birds, birds, everywhere. Note here how well Pied Crow's morbid humor and my own negotiation combined for success.

Deceased loved ones of the discarnate soul

The spirits that show up most commonly, invited or not, are the deceased loved ones of the stuck soul coming from the Other Side. Their aim is to encourage the soul to cross over, and they are very effective at this because of the soul's love and respect for them. These souls may be family members, professional colleagues, fellow soldiers, and so on. In the following case a deceased relative appeared.

Bahrain revolution 2011.

To an abandoned jeep in the middle of nowhere, where I saw a 30 year-old man who was trying to start the vehicle but was very frustrated. He told me, "It won't start!"

I asked, "Do you know why?" He said no, and I asked, "What's the last thing you remember?"

He said, "Soldiers drove up to me and made me stop and pulled out their guns and shot."

I asked if he was still alive, and he said, "I guess so."

So I asked, "Then where's your body?" That confused him, so I pointed to a spot some yards away, and when he saw the body he started crying. I said, "Your days in the physical world are over—did you have a good life?" He said he had had a very good one, so I asked if he was thankful. He paused and said yes. I said, "I can take you to another life now." He said he wasn't sure. I asked, "Do you know anyone who died that you'd like to see?"

He said, "My mother."

I pointed to Beautiful Warrior and said, "She can bring your mother here—if she does, will you go back with her?"

He agreed, and Beautiful Warrior left and brought back a woman in her fifties who was wearing black Muslim garb with a head covering, and the two left together.

Note in this case the efficacy of the "gratitude attitude," plus cool negotiation, combined with plucking the heartstrings of filial love. The next case involves compatriot spirit walk-ins.

Burma cyclone 2008.

To the land of the Karen where I saw an old man in his thirties who had been killed on the coast but then brought back to his homeland where he died because of lack of medical care. His soul was hovering over his grave in a Christian cemetery. He said he was staying there to find out why he had died so young.

I said, "Maybe it was to show the corruption and incompetence of the military dictatorship," and he got visibly animated. I said I could take him to a better place where other deceased souls are helping Burma's people free themselves. As we went to the Light, other Karen souls came out to greet him.

Deceased loved ones from the Other Side, then, are a welcome site, not just for the souls, but for the psychopomp as well since they always lend a helpful hand.

Mythic Psychopomp Spirits

Once in a while I enlist the power of ancient mythic spirits of various cultures around the world who are especially experienced in psychopomp work. In the case below, I asked the mythic psychopomp spirit Berchta to guide my journey.

Typhoon Haiyan 2013.

To the Philippines where Berchta took me to a male body trapped in rubble, but there was no soul around. The smell of death was everywhere. I asked her to take me to the man's soul, whereupon she led me to a middle-aged businessman 30 miles away. We then took him to the Other Side.

.

Unannounced power animals

A certain psychopomp story tells of two Light beings showing up unannounced and taking a despairing suicide victim to the Other Side. Near-death experiencers too encounter unearthly beings in nonordinary reality. The shaman, it is worth repeating, has to be ready and open for anything. The following case, involving the appearance of an unknown power animal, took me totally by surprise.

Haiti earthquake 2010.

Right away Crafty Canine jumped on me and said, "Stay close." I didn't realize just how close until later in the journey. Crafty Canine then took me outside of Port au Prince and I was drawn to a village where an old woman was looking at the ground.

"I was injured in Port au Prince but there was no medical treatment there, so some people brought me home to be cared for, but I didn't want to live." She told me she knew was dead, and added, "I don't care." I asked why.

"My life has been miserable, so why should the next one be any better?"

I said, "There are a lot of beautiful things everywhere, you just need to open your eyes." At that moment, unexpectedly, a spirit in the form of a big colorful parrot appeared and the woman's eyes lit up.

Parrot then asked her, "Would you like to fly with me?"

The woman asked, "How can I do that?"

Parrot pointed a wing at Crafty Canine and said, "Watch him." Crafty Canine then came up to me and jumped inside, merging completely—I was now a werecanine.

Then Parrot did the same to the woman, and asked her, "Want to see the Other Side now?" She agreed, and they flew off to the Light.

Birds, birds, everywhere. Note how Parrot, with its symbolic bright hues of joy, overcame the woman's dark despair.

Not-so-imaginary friends

During childhood I may have had "imaginary friends" from nonordinary reality, but I don't remember any, nor do many other adults, since such memories are effectively socialized out of us at a very young age. Yet researchers have found that children are especially sensitive to discarnates. Up to one-half of college students admit to having had "imaginary playments." Still, it came as some surprise when I saw how very relaxed living children can be when a spirit shows up, uninvited and unannounced, and can be clearly seen by them.

Indonesian tsunami 2004.

To a woman in her mid-twenties who was lying in mud and looking very sad. Her body was nowhere around. As I was puzzling over this, she told me, "I can't find my son."

I asked, "Will you go to the Light if I find him?" She agreed.

Crafty Canine then took me to Australia to a newlywed couple who had been honeymooning earlier on the Indonesian coast when the tsunami struck, and they felt very sorry for the victims. They then saw the boy in a refugee camp and wanted to adopt him, but were told that it was necessary to verify first that the boy's mother had actually died. They had already traveled again to Indonesia to the place where the boy had last seen her, but the body could not be found, so they had been unable to adopt him formally.

I was perplexed, wondering why the boy hadn't actually seen her body. Crafty Canine then took me back to Indonesia off the coast where it showed me some wreckage in the water under which the mother had been trapped and drowned—that was why the boy hadn't been able to find her body. I returned to the deceased mother in the mud and told her I had found her son, but she wanted to see for herself if he was OK.

Crafty Canine then took us all to Australia where the boy was playing in the yard of the newlyweds who had managed somehow to be allowed to care for him. The deceased mother told us, "I want him to know I'm OK and happy."

I knew that young children were able to interact with spirits, aka "imaginary friends," so I told her, "You may be able to appear to him and show him just that." She did, and he smiled as he watched us go up to the Light.

I realized here that, while I don't remember any childhood "imaginary friends," now I *am* one. Spirits, spirits, everywhere, and one of them is *me*.

The Crying Way

Nonordinary reality is the realm of the deep, especially very deep emotions, so it often elicits profound feelings in all concerned—shaman, client, and even observers. When such emotions are surrendered, renewed well-being occurs. In particular, the release of long-held grief has profound healing consequences. Shamanism, as Michael

Harner noted, is sometimes called "The Crying Way." As another of my teachers, Tom Brown, Jr., put it, "Never trust a shaman who can't cry." I encountered crying in almost 3 out of 10 episodes (29%). Perhaps the shaman should bring tissues along on every journey, or else look for other work.

In the following case, the surrender of pent-up emotions surrounding a lifetime of unresolved issues unleashed a torrent of tears.

Cincinnati Mercy Hospital 2010s.

To the emergency room where a middle-aged man, a suicide victim, was sitting next to a wall. Before he died, he had suffered from depression, lost his business in the 2008 economic collapse, and cheated on his wife. He knew he was dead but didn't think there was anything better in the future.

"Why do you believe that earthly reality is the only reality?" I asked. He couldn't answer. I said, "Do you think that maybe you're stuck here because you didn't deal with issues during your life on earth?" He begrudgingly agreed. I said, "On the Other Side there are compassionate and understanding beings who will help you to work out those issues."

At that point, Crafty Canine took the cuff of the man's shirtsleeve in its teeth and started tugging him toward the Light, whereupon the man collapsed and started crying. When he finished, Crafty Canine took his cuff again.

"I had a dog once," he said.

"Now you have one again!" I said, and the man started laughing and left for the Other Side.

Tibetan psychopomps, it is said, weep for days after seeing so much suffering in the other reality. So, while keeping a cool head, the shaman needs to draw on a warm heart.

The shamanic path, then, is not only the Laughing Way but also the Crying Way. The tragicomic mask of the theater might be an apt symbol for the craft. After all, it is said, the gods only *have to* listen to us on two occasions—when we laugh and when we cry. A river of tears—of joy and sorrow—brings us ordinary reality humans and those nonordinary reality gods together.

Energy Body Changes

Often dramatic changes, especially in color and luminosity, occur in the energy body of the discarnate soul, which signal to the shaman where the real problems lie, which emotions to key in on, and the extent to which progress is being made. For example, although shamans and other clairvoyants work with their own unique color schemes, they not uncommonly see gray and black for despair, grief, disappointment, and guilt; red for aggression, hate, anger, and revenge; blue for calm but also uncertainty, doubt, and indecision; and gold and white for peace, anticipation, joy, inspiration, gratitude, love, and purpose. In fact, up to one-half of palliative caregivers have seen a bright light surrounding dying persons. Little wonder that Andean shamans say about the afterlife: "We can only return dressed as light." For good reason, then, the energy body is sometimes called the "rainbow body."

I noticed dramatic energy body changes in 9% of the episodes. They included brightening of the eyes; color changes in the aura; glowing and beaming; and otherwise a coming alive with a light of some kind.

David Kowalewski, PhD

U.S. invasion of Iraq 2003.

To Baghdad to the bombed-out Bath Party headquarters, where I saw an official, surrounded by a disturbing red aura, staring at the rubble. I figured it was unwise to approach him as an American, so I asked a helping spirit to ask him, "What's wrong."

"I hate the USA and Saddam for what they did to my country."

My helping spirit asked, "Is it hate, or is it grief for what you've lost and guilt for how you supported Saddam?" At the word grief, he burst out crying and my helping spirit offered him its neck to cry on. He cried for five minutes, by the end of which his aura had turned blue.

My helping spirit said, "Now, about that guilt—there's an American here who also feels guilty—will you listen to him?"

He agreed, and I said, "I'm truly sorry at what the USA did and how we were lied to—I'm very, very sorry." At this we both started crying and soon were hugging.

He said, "I'm sorry we Iraqis didn't have enough courage to get rid of Saddam ourselves."

I said, "OK, but that's all in the past. If you let me take you to the Light, I promise to work on Americans on earth."

He objected, "Why can't I stay on earth?"

I said, "The problem is spiritual—you're pure spirit now, without that heavy body to carry around, so you can do much more powerful work in the spirit world."

He smiled at the logic and said, "I'm ready." By now his aura had turned golden-white, and he left for the Other Side.

What if the world's leaders were taught to read auras? Just a thought …

Symbols

I used to wonder at my personal fascination with symbols, even choosing them for the topic of my doctoral dissertation and later research. Now I understand. Nonordinary reality, as the wisdom traditions have recognized for millennia, is saturated with symbols, and the shaman who ignores that fact is, to that extent, ineffective. In shamanic journeys, symbols come out of nowhere, or better, out of the Big Everywhere.

Bosnia war 1995.

To a hut with seven women inside who had been gang-raped, and a Serbian soldier who had been killed right after the rape and was holding them captive. He refused to free them.

So Beautiful Warrior started flying around the soldier, who fired shots but the bullets all missed. Crafty Canine then lunged and grabbed the soldier's crotch in its jaws, whereupon I told the two to go outside and wait.

I then asked the women why they were still there and they said, "We're feeling shameful, because in some way we enjoyed it."

I said, "It's natural to enjoy sex, so you don't have to feel shame."

Then Beautiful Warrior arranged them in a circle holding hands and said, "Each of you look at the others and see how beautiful you all are." They did so and started laughing. Then a pillar of white light came into the center of the circle, which they entered and then climbed up to the Other Side.

I then went outside to the soldier, who didn't want to go to the Light because he didn't want to face the judgment of

God or other deceased humans. I said, "You were a warrior of the body—why can't you be a warrior of the spirit now?"

He lit up and said, "I guess I can."

I said, "I don't know what's there, but you need to face the music like a brave soldier."

He agreed, whereupon Crafty Canine released its grip. The soldier then walked up to the Light, limping slowly.

The symbolism in this case was comically rich. I couldn't help but think, "We've got him by the balls now" as Crafty Canine grabbed the soldier, and, "The soldier got his balls back," as the journey ended. The soldier had misused his testicles to attack the women's genitalia, so Crafty Canine provided a free attitude adjustment right at that part of the body. Crafty Canine then only released its grip when the soldier got his courage, namely "his balls," back. I suppose you can "make this stuff up," as the saying goes, but personally I don't have that kind of talent.

Thanks and No Thanks

Since psychopomp work doesn't pay well, at least it's nice to feel appreciated once in a while. The most grateful actors during the journeys, I've found, are the discarnate souls themselves.

Congolese civil war 2012.

To a village massacre site where I saw a middle-aged man with gray hair lying bloody on his side with his top arm outstretched and begging not to be slain. He was obviously frozen in time and didn't realize he'd been killed.

I knelt beside him and told him it was too late to save himself, and tried to lift him up, but his body was too heavy with grief at what had happened to his village. I told him to put his head on my shoulder and pour out all his sorrow through his eyes and onto the ground, otherwise he would be "grounded" there, suffering for a long time. He did so and eventually started to rise, which I took advantage of by guiding him right to the Light.

Before entering, he turned and I saw that all the suffering was gone from his eyes, which had now become fierce with life. He said, "What can I do for you?" I said that something dark was harassing me.

He turned me around, put his head directly behind my right shoulder, and whispered in my ear, "I've got your back now." Then he entered the Light.

But some souls, despite the psychopomp's efforts, opt not to go to the Light for a number of reasons, as happened in 8% of the episodes. Here's one example.

Pakistan earthquake 2013.

To a valley with lots of collapsed houses where I saw a 6 year-old boy looking lost. I asked, "Do you know what earthquakes are?" He didn't, so I explained that they take a lot of people away to another place, but that the people who go away can still see us here on earth.

He was anxious about being unable to find his parents, so we started looking for his mother who was usually at home but she was not there. So we went around to the neighbors' houses and Crafty Canine, in his cadaver dog role, sniffed out her body under some rubble. I told the boy she had gone to that other place and would like him to join her.

But he said he needed to find his father too. We went into town looking for his father's workplace, asking some spirits there where it was, and we found him there, alive and working. I asked the boy if he would like to join his mother now. He declined, saying that his father needed him to help with chores.

I told him that he wouldn't be able to help in that previous way but could stay if he wanted to, but that he shouldn't disturb his father at all. He agreed and seemed happy to be with his father. I told him that if he ever needs me he can just call Crafty Canine and I'll come, especially if he wants to go to his mother.

In a similar case, the compassion of a group of men led them to graciously turn down our psychopomp offer.

New Hampshire State Prison 1890s.

Fully expecting to meet some sort of psychopathic serial killer, I was surprised when five smiling inmates came up and greeted us right away. They had been convicted of murder, but then reformed themselves and decided to band together to help other prisoners, such as protecting them from bullying, extortion, and so on. Their work was so successful when they were alive that they decided to continue it after death.

"So," I said, "you want to stay." They said yes. I wanted to know how they were able to help the current prisoners.

"We combine our five energies into one, and that always overcomes the wrongdoers." We wished them well and left.

Later, I was gratified to learn that deceased souls do indeed form teams to better intervene in our ordinary reality. Social life continues after death.

A comparable "no thanks" case involved a "witch doctor" soul who wanted to continue his service.

South Sudan conflict 2014.

To a refugee camp where a deceased old man with gray hair was lying on a cot. He greeted us and said he wanted to stay around to help his people.

I asked, "How can you do that? You don't have a body."

He said, "I don't need one. I just dial down my vibrations to the earthly level, then envision my energy body materializing into a physical body in the greatest detail, then envision the words I want to say, then with the strongest intent speak them into the ear of the person needing help."

I realized that he was a "witch doctor," a shaman, of great experience and compassion, and that I had been led here to learn from him. "How do you help?" I asked.

"I start by lifting their spirits, but in this desperate situation the best way to do that is to tell them how to get basic necessities like food, water, and security."

I left, humbled.

Souls are also likely to refuse crossing over if they died with some sort of obsessive disorder. The following case illustrates the problem.

Ukrainian fascist putsch 2014.

I went with mythic spirit Odin to Kiev to the central square, whereupon he said, "Wait here." He returned with a middle-aged woman who had been killed when she tried to help her husband who had been shot. Her husband later died. She knew she was dead but didn't want to go to the Other Side. Odin then left again and returned with her deceased husband, a Ukrainian nationalist who had been demonstrating and wanted to keep fighting against the democratic government.

I tried to convince him to cross over, but he kept looking down, a crazed blood-lust in his eyes, and wouldn't even look up at me. Odin gave me a look as if to say, "Don't push it."

So I tried to convince his wife to cross over, but she said, "I have to look after him so he won't do anything stupid." I asked Odin if he could look after the man, and he agreed.

But she was skeptical and asked, "How do I know he can do that?"

Odin then morphed into Crafty Canine, at which she was shocked and said, "OK I'll go!" She departed, leaving her husband behind.

Later I realized that Odin, Norse warrior god who serves fallen soldiers in his Valhalla hall, had brought me a deceased *berserker* fighter to deal with. At that point I wished I *could* "make this stuff up."

Timmy. A friend once emailed me, asking if I would do a long-distance healing journey for his friend's young son who was dying from leukemia in a hospital. I got out my drum and did a soul-flight there with Native-American. But when we arrived Native-American said, "Don't do anything." I was confused—why had we come here in the first place then? As I was about to ask Native-American, the boy's energy body suddenly arose from his physical body and glowed with an intense and radiant golden light. He said, "I need to die so I can help my father from the Other Side." Five months later, I met my friend one night and asked him about Timmy. He said Timmy was still alive. Then I

told him my journey story. Early the next morning my friend ran up to me and said, "Timmy just died last night." Was Timmy speaking to us from the beyond? You decide.

CHAPTER 9

Real or Make-Believe?

Earthquake. It was the middle of the night and I was sleeping at my home in the Montana Rockies, when I bolted upright in bed, opened my eyes, and saw a vision of a huge neon sign flashing, "Earthquake! Earthquake!" which then disappeared. At that point my fort-like log home started shaking so violently that it was tossing me around in my bed. When the shaking stopped, I went back to sleep. Next morning I turned on the news and heard for the first time about the Haiti earthquake that had killed thousands. But what about the earthquake I had felt the night before? I listened to the local news—nothing. I checked for damage to the house, inside and out—nothing. I asked the townsfolk if they had felt anything—nothing. I waited for an aftershock—nothing. I checked online for any seismic activity in the area—nothing. But *something* had happened.

How might we know that psychopomps in fact escort souls to the Other Side? Personally, as someone trained and experienced in the scientific method, I take such questions seriously and go out of my way to publish on the topic, even devoting special sections in my articles to the *reasonable* doubts of *truth-seeking* skeptics. Such skeptics are to be honored, since they keep us shamanic practitioners honest and sharp.

Still, it's hard to prove that psychopomp work is in fact a reality and not simply make-believe, hallucination, delusion, wishful thinking, or charlatanism. Compared to some shamanic practices, like healing a broken leg with a mere touch, it is very subtle, and most action takes place in nonordinary reality. Yet, through careful and thorough preparation and follow-up, some evidence for its veracity can be gathered. Ideally, such evidence is collected and witnessed by many independent, competent, ethical, and experienced observers over a period of time.

Psychopomps themselves have an interest in assembling such evidence. Even experienced shamans have bad days, and so traditional peoples have had no problem saying that a medicine person has "lost the power." Competent professionals, as well, always fact-check their work. Also, if the work is unsuccessful, discarnate souls, who may be malevolent, may follow the psychopomp home, and so it's in the psychopomp's own interest to make sure the job is done well.

Shake Rattle, and Roll

Here's a dramatic example from the earthquake happening described in the story at the beginning of this chapter. That night's experience told me I had better put on my psychopomp hat and get to work. "No shake," say the Micmac, "no shaman." Also, dreams related to death in any way need to be taken seriously.

So, I started shaking my rattle and told my helping spirits, "Let's roll!" and added, "to save a doggone soul." Little did I know we'd wind up at Heartbreak Hotel.

Haiti earthquake 2010.

To the rubble of the Montana Hotel in Port au Prince where Crafty Canine went into cadaver dog mode and sniffed out two people, an aid worker and his Haitian mistress, and then another, a European mother whose child was missing. We found the child and asked if it wanted to see its mom, and it said yes, so we reunited them. Then Crafty Canine found a Haitian waiter. We put the five into the Magic Sled and Crafty Canine pulled them to the Light.

Crafty Canine quickly returned and led me to a collapsed office building. It started pawing frantically at the rubble, but then ran off and came back with a living policeman, who removed the larger pieces of rubble, revealing the waving hand of a living young woman, a secretary who had been buried alive.

Montana Hotel? Please, I thought after this journey, no way—the demon of doubt was attacking me big time. I disbelieved that any Montana Hotel even existed in Haiti, since I couldn't imagine any two places more different than the Montana Rockies and that country, and since alphanumerics like names tend to be rarely found in nonordinary reality. I suspected, then, that the ordinary-reality memory of my dream in Montana the night before had somehow leaked into my consciousness to contaminate my nonordinary-reality journey.

So, I embarked on a major fact-checking expedition to debunk my own journey. I googled the name Montana Hotel and Haiti earthquake, and to my astonishment found that the structure did in fact exist, or I should say existed, since during the quake the 5-story main building had pancaked, killing dozens. One of the surviving guests, I found out too, even wrote a book about the event, which I found listed on amazon.com. Here I have to add that I had never been to Haiti, much less heard of the Montana Hotel, let alone read the book about the disaster. It was all news to me.

The authenticity of this journey, proven by the fact-checking, also gave me some general clues about what to look for when assessing if "I made it all up." Namely, my journeys with Crafty Canine, especially when it shows up with its Magic Sled, are good signs that they are for real. The experience also told me that when dramatic dreams tell of some kind of tragedy, subsequent journeys to the site or to the deceased soul(s) that appeared in those dreams are for real. It is this process of shifting back and forth between ordinary and nonordinary realities, I realized too, that over time makes for a powerful psychopomp.

Other Ways of Knowing

This Haiti case was especially dramatic. Usually, though, the proof is in a far more subtle pudding. Yet many such types of supporting evidence for authenticity can easily be found.

{} **Feelings.** Often, at the moment when a soul crosses to the Other Side from a haunted site, shamans and observers "feel" a lightening up of the place, "feel" less oppressed, no longer "feel" someone is watching them, and so on. Traditional peoples have respected these sensations, but modern ones are far more skeptical. When communicating with modern peoples, then, smart psychopomps might do well to avoid using any such "feelings" as "proof," if only to avoid raised eyebrows. They themselves, though, can gauge authenticity by the depth, intensity, and sudden change in feelings.

{} **Contradiction of expectations**. Unknown and unlikely information is sometimes made available during journeys that contradicts expectation, especially "scientific" prognosis, but later proves true. Here's an example.

Tropical storm Sendong 2011.

To Davao in the Philippines where a young woman was floating above a refugee shelter crying and saying that she could no longer take care of her 6 year-old living daughter who was all alone.

I told her I have powerful spirit allies who will look after her daughter until the child can take care of herself. Beautiful Warrior then sat down next to the girl and put her arm around her to comfort her, Crafty Canine stood in front of her to protect her, and Morbid Corvid 1 hovered above her looking in all directions for any danger. The woman then looked visibly relieved and went with me to the Light.

I had been a Fulbright scholar in the Philippines in the 1980s and experienced some storms of my own there. But this journey seemed strange because Davao, I knew, has the reputation of being a "typhoon-free zone." So the demon of doubt was attacking me again. But later, when I fact-checked my journey by googling tropical storms in the Philippines, I found out that indeed one had hit Davao in 2011, leaving 150,000 displaced. I was sure, then, that the young woman had been a victim of the storm and her daughter one of the displaced.

Here are three more scenarios. Imagine an apparent death that just occurred and the psychopomp journeys to the soul, only to find out that it is just in a state of temporary unconsciousness and in fact is not dead. He reports this to family and friends and healthcare providers, who find it to be true when the patient revives.

Imagine that a psychopomp journeys to a recently departed soul and brings back to surviving loved ones information from the soul that only they knew.

Imagine that a psychopomp brings back from souls information that was unknown, such as new facts about their deaths, about certain historical events, or about the location of buried artifacts—information that is later verified.

{} **Internal consistency.** I'm often amazed at how the details of a journey, which usually occurs with lightning speed, are later seen to fit together into a coherent whole. For example, the case of the strangled wife showed the consistency between the constant nagging of the wife and the way her husband expressed his frustration—he took a simple and direct, albeit drastic, means to silence her. The professional psychopomp, then, carefully reviews every case for "factual fit."

{} **Revelations from the deceased to survivors about the crossing over.** The discarnate soul who has crossed over may manifest to survivors, in full-body apparitions or vivid dreams or other ways, telling them that the psychopomp has taken it to a place of peace on the Other Side, yet they do not find out until later about the psychopomp or the work that was done.

{} **End of disturbances after de-haunting.** In cases of hauntings of structures, the disturbances may end immediately after psychopomps have done their work. Ideally, empirical evidence for the disturbances was captured on instruments prior to the psychopomp work, and then the sites were measured for the same phenomena right afterwards. Ideally, the disturbances were experienced by multiple observers at the same time.

But a caveat is in order. Such dramatic changes would be *consistent* with the hypothesis of successful psychopomp work, but are hardly *proof*, because of the scientific dictum: Absence of evidence is not evidence of absence. The discarnate soul may have simply decided to stop manifesting in ordinary reality, to "lay low" for another day. It may have left to haunt another place, only to return later. Thus, in order to further support their claims, competent psychopomps need to seek out long-term follow-up information.

But a reverse caveat is also in order: A continuation of disturbances does not necessarily mean a psychopomp failure. Possibly there were two or more souls manifesting, and the psychopomp was given information on, and access to, only one. Or, a new disruptive soul may have come to the site right after the work. Or, a powerful living shaman may have been "bilocating" (that is, acting as a *Doppelgänger*) there and creating disruptions much like a discarnate soul. Thus, professional psychopomps attempt to find out the total number of spirits active at a site before proceeding with the work. Such preparation increases the likelihood that all the souls who want to cross over are helped to do so, and that the ones who do not either leave or stop disturbing the clients. Later, psychopomps can check that no new souls are disturbing the site.

In cases of possession, the disturbed behaviors of the victim may end immediately, and preferably a qualified psychologist has documented such behaviors before the psychopomp work and their absence after it. But again the caveat: Absence of evidence is not evidence of absence. And again, continued strange behavior may be caused by another, unseen, possessor or by a new one that just arrived, and so does not invalidate the original successful depossession by the psychopomp.

{} **Dramatic exits.** In some cases, dramatic and inexplicable loud "pops" or bright lights or strong winds manifest at the moment the psychopomp escorts the soul to the Other Side, followed by total peace and quiet.

{} **Corroboration from mediums.** Experienced clairvoyants may "see" the psychopomp escorting the discarnate soul away and later reveal details of the crossing over, which the psychopomp then confirms. Also, since shamans can have bad days, they do well to seek confirmation from those who are especially skilled at sensing spirits. The greater the number of competent clairvoyants reporting the presence or absence of a deceased soul, the better. A shamanic axiom, after all, is that collective work is almost always more powerful than individual effort.

{} **Corroboration from other journeying shamans.** Fellow psychopomps may experience the same activities at the same site at the same time. This kind of evidence cuts little ice among skeptics, but is very rewarding for the psychopomp. Here's an example.

U.S. invasion of Vietnam 1968.

Together with 25 other shamanic practitioners I journeyed on behalf of a fellow practitioner, a Vietnam veteran, to a battlefield where many of his buddies had been killed. I came across a Vietnamese soldier who didn't want to cross over.

"I want to keep fighting," he said, and I felt a huge wall of incomprehension rise up between us. He would have nothing to do with my offer.

So I returned to ordinary reality, feeling I had somehow failed at moving him to the Other Side.

But I was wrong. During the narrations of our individual journeys, I heard three of the other practitioners say that they had also met Vietnamese soldiers and hit the same kind of wall. No one had crossed a single one over. I was relieved, and couldn't resist thumbing my nose at the demon of doubt.

{} **Corroboration from paranormal scientists.** After many a journey, I've come across accounts by paranormal researchers that have validated my strange experiences. For example, I was a bit skeptical about seeing the golden white light around souls just as they were going to the Other Side, since it seemed way too close to the halos in European paintings of the saints—in other words my own projection. But later, when I started reading about afterlife communications of souls to their survivors, I found that the deceased often manifest bathed in such a light. Skeptics may say that, in fact, I had read those accounts *before* my journeys, but I, and other practitioners I respect, know how to tell time.

In sum, every psychopomping effort may yield some kind information that will keep the shaman working and the skeptics from closing their minds down completely. Still, the demon of doubt kept harassing me about one thing: Crafty Canine's Magic Sled, which just seemed too ... well ... *convenient,* not to mention way too much like a projection of Santa Clause's famous vehicle.

But then I came across an ethnographic account of a Chukchi shaman who sang about his journeys: "My beloved reindeer … I yoke … to the sledge." Coincidence? Or synchronicity? You decide. As for me, I've stopped believing in Santa Clause, but not in Crafty Canine.

JonBenet 1. Tired of hearing about innocent people being imprisoned and executed, I began wondering why we weren't using all our paranormal tools to "get it right." So I offered a course at my university called Psychic Policing. I was happy, then, when the students started doing well, especially in remote-viewing, namely soul-flights to some earthly site in nonordinary reality. When their average score for practice exercises hit about 60%, I decided to let them cut their teeth on a real crime. I chose the JonBenet Ramsey case, since the publicity offered a wealth of detail allowing us to fact-check our work. Before class I went to the library to get a photocopy of her to serve as the students' concealed "target" for the remote-viewing. I grabbed some thick bound tomes of weekly news magazines off the shelves and, distracted, tossed them on a table and randomly opened one up. JonBenet's face popped up immediately on the front cover of the opened issue. Coincidence? Maybe, but I took it as a sign.

CHAPTER 10

What the Dead Can Teach the Living

JonBenet 2. JonBenet, a 6 year-old blonde girl, had been sexually violated and murdered, hit on the head and strangled, the body being found in her basement bedroom, which was full of dolls and stuffed animals, at her three-story brick house in Boulder in the Colorado Rockies on Christmas day in 1996. A ransom note hinted at a botched kidnapping attempt. I came back from the library, put the photocopy in a sealed envelope, and walked into the classroom. I tossed the envelope on the seminar table and told the students to remote-view the scene of "this unsolved crime that occurred somewhere in the world sometime in the past 10 years" and to gather as much evidence as possible. I started drumming and 20 minutes later they revealed their "data." The six students who did fairly well got these hits: (1) cold; snow; mountain peaks; (2) headache; pointy peaks; man-made structure; three-stories; (3) cold; white; soft; ski lift; Colorado mountains; waterfalls; peaks; (4) hilly;

man-made structure; igloo; tundra; Alaska or Arctic; (5) three stories of a home; chilly; hill; (6) white sidewalk outside; waterfall; cold; house; (6) house with chimney; scared; go away; child; cry; screams; tired people who lost a child, a girl; very sad; mid-America. Then there were the three students who did better.

After completing dozens of psychopomp journeys, I realized that I too was benefiting from the work. For example, I learned that living children really do see spirits, aka "imaginary friends"; in fact, there is nothing imaginary about them. In short, psychopomps evolve to greater wisdom and power as they practice their craft. There are, I've come to understand, not only ghosts needing psychopomps, but psychopomps needing ghosts.

Yet the notion that the living can learn from the dead seems absurd to many, who fail to realize the permeability of the veil between ordinary and nonordinary realities. Also, not only do many of the living not want to think about death at all, but they see longevity as success and death as failure, so why would they want to listen to such "losers"?

But I've learned that the dead have not only some useful tips for the living, but even profound lessons about how to live one's entire life. Having "been there" during my near-death experience and psychopomp journeys, I've found that the deceased can tell us how death can inform life, and how living well predicts dying well. If you want to learn about life, listen to the dead.

Lessons for Us All

Some deep philosophy comes from deceased souls that applies to your life. They have a lot to teach you about a number of topics. Here is what they are saying.

{} **Facing the music.** Acknowledge death, and deal with it, now. A philosophy joke goes: "God is dead."—Nietzsche ... "Nietzsche is dead."—God. Ceremonialize death by role-playing the short period just before your death, the moment of death itself, the funeral or other last rite, and the grieving of your survivors. If now you care more about your iPhone than your immortal soul, you may have a big shock down the road. To avoid getting earthbound after death, accept death in all its reality now. A good practice is to envision your death every day. How do you want to be when you die? As philosopher Martin Heidegger put it, the human is a *Sein-an-Tod*, a being-towards-death, that is, one's whole life should be geared towards one's state at that last moment. Meet death head-on, dead-on.

{} **Doing your homework.** Imagine you have to travel—absolutely necessarily—to a place on the other side of the world, but instead of coming home you have to stay there forever. Wouldn't you check out that place beforehand? So, research the afterlife—you're going to be there a long time. There are many excellent scientific studies about near-death experiences—learn about them. To claim, "I don't believe in an afterlife," without looking at all the scientific research on the topic is all too reminiscent of geocentrists and evolution-deniers. Death is *not* "the great unknown." Millions of people over thousands of years have left us volumes and volumes of information. We just need to do our homework While knowledge about life may make us smart, knowledge about death makes us wise. Just realize that the deeper you dig into the Big Mystery, the more mysterious it gets.

{} **Deleting "What-ever!"** Closing your eyes to the afterlife, by disregarding its importance and especially by denying it, can lead to despair, the most important negative binding of discarnate souls to the earthly plane in my journeys. Despair, in fact, is far more prevalent in earthly life than popularly acknowledged. Routinely it is not dealt with, but instead treated as "depression" and pharmacologized. But in fact it is an existential crisis that can be overcome by a leap of courage and curiosity. For those in despair, an opening up to the possibility of an afterlife and an exploration of the evidence for its reality is a far more effective therapy than taking pills. The denial of the afterlife and the denial of life are too often the same denial.

{} **Detaching.** At death the discarnate soul becomes a wayfarer for whom the previous earthly life was just one leg of a longer journey. Death marks the point at which you take off your old clothes and put on the new. It is a finality but also a beginning, and so is a transition point, a springboard from which you cross over from an old way of being to a new one. As such, it needs to be seen as a liberation from the confines and limitations of the body and a springboard to new possibilities, to new powers, to new experiences. Death is an opening and not just a closing. So start letting go of your material attachments now, while you still can—detach! You literally "can't take it with you." Hearses don't have luggage racks. I once heard a man exclaim, "Whoever dies with the most toys wins!" to which his wife retorted, "Whoever dies with the most toys is dead!"

But detachment is not uncaring. Attachment springs from need, based on dependent powerlessness, while caring springs from love, based on independent power. Our earthly job, then, is to write our own declaration of spiritual independence and so empower ourselves by returning to Source who wants us home free. Freeing ourselves before death enhances freedom afterwards. Cling to nothing. The most important word in spirituality is *surrender*.

Especially avoid attaching to revenge, anger, hatred— these may well "haunt you" in the afterlife. Forgiveness now is postmortem health later. The freer you are at death, the faster you'll fly in the afterlife.

The psychopomp, then, is truly a spiritual freedom-fighter, telling us to liberate ourselves from all bindings— to a cause, institution, family, drugs, alcohol, material goods, and so on. Aspiring psychopomps, then, would do well to research obsession, compulsion, fixation, addiction, dependency, co-dependency, and similar psychospiritual bonds.

{} **Lightening up.** The flip side of detachment is weightlessness. In my journeys I've been struck by the heaviness of the discarnate soul's energy body that literally seems pressed down by concerns. Occupants of haunted buildings as well feel a "heaviness" in the air. But when we realize that every death is a new beginning, we can rejoice at the baby! We are mortal for a reason. As a young man I used to visit hospice patients as part of my church's ministry, a task I immediately dreaded when I first heard the assignment. "Who wants to hang out with old dying people?" I thought secretly. But I was quickly disabused of that notion, finding that almost all of the patients radiated a glorious kind of peace and grace and beauty, an incredible lightness of being. I thought that the world's creative intelligentsia should start portraying the beautiful side of death in painting, dance, literature, and so on. I was also reminded of Egyptian lore which says that after death you will be judged by having your heart weighed against a feather: If it weighs more, you lose. So, the dead tell us, "Lighten up and you win." Think: feather!

{} **Living ethically.** Live ethically, not because some cleric told you to do so under pain of social opprobrium or eternal hellfire, but because otherwise you may well have a miserable afterlife. You may stay stuck, in a time-freeze. Dante's genius in the *Divine Comedy* was to place Satan, not hopping in a cauldron of boiling oil, but frozen in a block of ice. In the wisdom traditions, it is self-absorption—psychospiritual narcissism—that keeps us frozen even here on earth. So psychopomps, not surprisingly, find many an earthbound soul in just that self-centered deep-freeze condition.

{} **Soul-tending.** Deal with your psychospiritual problems now. Do the deep soul work. Care for your soul like a garden—dig out the weeds. Thoroughly become who you want to be at the moment of death. Heal your wounds now by deeply grieving, or you will be earthbound at death, heavy with grief and anger and revenge. Cry now so you won't have to later. Stop self-indulgence in controlled substances. Addiction you will have to deal with sooner or later. Don't wait for, or expect, some kind of deathbed salvation. Spiritually speaking, "as in life, so in death," "as below, so above." If your life is a "living hell" now, why should it be any better after death? Deal with your hell on earth. If you are weak at death, you'll be weak afterwards. Deal with your hang-ups in this life so they won't hang you up in the next. Empower your soul now, before you die, so you can move to higher levels of power and wisdom.

{} **Carpe diem.** Near-death experiencers and discarnate souls teach us not to fear death, in order that we can "seize the day"—live life to the full. "Give strength to the intensity of your life," advised Chamalú, an Andean shaman, "so that … death … does not find you already dead." "A full life," he concluded, "is the passport to eternity." The less the fear of death, the less the fear of life. So Socrates got it wrong: It's not the unexamined life that's not worth living, it's the unlived life that's not worth examining. Live as if there is no tomorrow—it may be true. If you don't, after death you'll be angry and regret that you never really lived. Don't wait till retirement to make a bucket list. If you live life to the full, then you can leave it without regrets. Longevity is not life—living is.

{} **Prepping.** "Doomsday preppers" are subject to widespread ridicule, especially by the arrogant and unprepared. Personally, with the exception of a tiny minority of clinical paranoids, I admire them. Earthbound souls, I learned, are in effect telling us to "get prepped." Clean up your earthly affairs. Stop procrastinating, make the difficult decisions, and take care of unfinished business. Pondering the possibility of imminent death is not an absurdity but a teaching moment. It's a wake-up call to get ready. Formally express your loves and regrets. Above all, forgive. The key question is: "When I die, will I be at peace?" Will you leave harmony in your wake? If not, you may well become a spiritual parasite on survivors.

Do all the last-days arrangements now, such as making a will and updating it regularly. Leave a clean highway behind you—don't litter. It may be a bit depressing now, but it can be far more so after death if you put it off.

Scheduling your own postmortem ceremony is a very good idea. But think in terms of a two-stage process, the first stage being a grieving death-rite to honor the sadness felt at the loved one's departure, but the next stage, after the mourning is over, being a celebratory birth-rite to honor the joy felt at the loved one's new life. Plan, then, for survivors to grieve the absence of the deceased in ordinary reality, but to celebrate its presence in nonordinary reality. Such a shamanic ceremony honors both the Crying Way and the Laughing Way. The soul, after all, in fact will have just been born into a new life, with a wealth of adventures to look forward to. In fact, we might all do well to celebrate "death birthdays" with even more festivity than "birth birthdays." Whereas birth merely kicks off a known-to-be-short leg of the soul's journey, death kicks off the mysterious eternal remainder. In sum, preparing for postmortem life is sound premortem advice.

Lessons for Survivors

Discarnate souls have special lessons for surviving loved ones.

{} **Ending the taboo.** When face to face with dying souls, everyone can do their part to prepare them for the afterlife. At least honor the possibility of one. If you've had a near-death experience, come out of the closet and tell everyone, in both private and public venues. Everyone can help to de-tabooize death and publicly honor it as the liberation it is. This will lessen the fear of death, which can be especially comforting for the terminally ill. The dying need to rejoice in their next adventure, not fear it.

Fear-mongering only increases the power of those who want to control our souls instead of freeing them.

{} **Deathbed shamanizing.** The ancient shaman offered deathbed services, to prepare the dying so they could make a smooth and graceful transition to the afterlife, and to console the soon-to-be survivors. Already shamans are helping patients in hospice care. True, having a modern shaman-psychopomp present at the time of death today may seem way too old-fashioned, to all, that is, except the souls themselves who can be helped to transit smoothly to the afterlife.

{} **Letting go.** Honor the deceased with a respectful ceremony immediately after their deaths, but then let them go so they can move on. Some psychics claim that one reason discarnate souls are earthbound is because survivors hold on to them, not wanting to admit reality, thereby causing the souls to feel guilty if they leave the earthly plane. So holding on to the deceased, like keeping a room "exactly as it was when X died," is in fact to reject a closure to the grieving process. Stubborn refusal to move on to new relationships and the like is just a bad idea.

{} **Keeping it real.** Please stop saying about the dead, "Oh, they're in a better place now." What "better place"? Are you sure? Unless you have psychopomp skills, you don't know that, so please stop saying it. The dead may in fact be in a miserable place, and the warning signs from their previous earthly lives are clear: denial of the afterlife, non-exemplary behavior, addiction, and so on. These are all clues that a psychopomp may be needed. Also, stop complaining about the "loss" of a loved one. You've lost nothing; they're still around, just in a different dimension of reality. Death is just a move from one reality to another, and you'll make that move yourself sooner or later, and maybe psychopomps will be around to make sure you reunite with those very loved ones.

Public Policy Implications

The Ghosts of Psychopomping Past, Present, and Future raise serious questions about the way we do public business. In particular, sudden and violent deaths live on far beyond the events themselves. Post-traumatic stress disorder is not just found in ordinary reality. In the current and coming global crises, we need policies that better prevent the deaths that keep souls earthbound.

Getting up to date on the "big data" that has been collected on global mortality is a good place to start. A huge proportion of premature deaths stem from *very preventable* roots. Such causes include insufficient attention to pollution, dangerous roadways, and the like.

The specifics of the needed policy changes are easy to find. More support for safe working conditions, emergency management, and search-and-rescue is needed. Early warning systems need overhauling. For example, the region of the ocean affected by the earthquake that caused the disastrous Asian tsunami in 2004 had no adequate seismographic system that could have saved thousands of lives. Likewise, the shameful response of the U.S. government to Hurricane Katrina left thousands stranded and dying. Simple maintenance of public infrastructure, such as levy renovation, bridge repair, and dam inspection, can easily avert many sudden and violent deaths around the world. So too can better prevention and early warning of avalanches, volcanic eruptions, tornadoes, forest fires, mudslides, mine cave-ins and explosions, plane crashes, train derailments, ship sinkings, floods, and epidemics. Better laws can save millions of lives; in the USA, a

55-mph speed limit alone could prevent 10,000-20,000 deaths from vehicle accidents a year.

Better suicide prevention measures could reduce the number of discarnate souls stuck in despair. Safer health measures, according to the prestigious *Journal of the American Medical Association*, could prevent hundreds of thousands of deaths from medication errors, unnecessary and botched surgeries, pharmaceutical side effects, and hospital infections. Tougher laws against sexual assault are a no-brainer—rape leaves souls traumatized not only during life but after it as well.

Controlling the production, storage, and spread of weapons of mass destruction, whether conventional or unconventional, is a must. These weapons almost seem to be saying that our disregard for the afterlife has led us into disregard for life itself. But can any sane person believe they make us more secure? Since democracies *virtually never* go to war against democracies, strong citizen control over national governments is a necessary place to start.

But international war is hardly the biggest violence problem. According to sophisticated global statistics, national governments kill *four times* more of *their own* people (aka "democide") than do foreigners. That is, you are much more likely to die a violent death at the hands of your own government than from any other agent. In the C20th alone, governments killed some 150 million of their own citizens. Genocide, politicide, ethnic cleansing, state terrorism, and the like may doom us all unless we impose strict citizen constraints on the governmental tools of violence everywhere. Fascism, physical and digital, is not an option.

Violent and other sudden deaths have a lot of earthly aftereffects, but the postmortem ones are usually ignored.

The results of such death can live on, in the form of haunted buildings and highways and possessed people, to include our own family members, coworkers, and neighbors. Such death is not good for you and me—or the dead. Unless we adopt the above policy measures, our foolishness will literally haunt us for a long, long time.

A Psychopomp Revival?

Is the shamanic renaissance just another spiritual fad? Or has it arisen because shamans are necessary for providing useful services? According to shamans, their skills are needed more than ever to treat the spiritual crisis of today, which lies at the root of our current environmental, political, and other serious disorders.

This is true especially of shamanic psychopomp work. Since restless discarnates are not good for you and me, the ancients did not just think it nice to help the dead cross over, but necessary. They did a simple cost-benefit analysis. They called on psychopomps to eliminate the costs of disruption and provide the benefits of healing and tranquility. Thus Charon and the other spirits who have been associated with navigating the realm of the dead were not simply fictional characters that traditionals mused about over campfires, but valuable social workers who kept the community healthy by bringing spiritual peace.

But today? Just do the math. Whereas world population tops seven billion with increasing millions dying each year, psychopomp work is rare. Should we then not expect a growing public attention to hosts of ghosts, including hauntings and possessions? Can the global community endure such an assault? That's the bad news.

The good news? Medical technology, combined with air evacuation and other emergency services, have brought back countless people from death, thereby increasing the pool of near-death experiencers and thus potential shamans and especially psychopomps. So in terms of sheer numbers, whereas psychopomp work is more needed than before, it is also more possible.

It seems more than just a bit justifiable, then, to speculate about a psychopomp revival in particular. Many possibilities come to mind. Could hospitals, in emergency facilities and operating rooms, employ psychopomps to help the newly departed cross over? In cases of possession, might healthcare institutions allow shamans to do exorcism work? Might war veterans with shamanic skills be trained to psychopomp their deceased buddies and enemies and civilian collateral damage? Already some coroners psychopomp a soul after its body has been prepared. Could shamans be on call to provide long-distance psychopomp services at sites of mass accidents and natural disasters? Could they open offices of professional grief counseling for survivors?

Special attention might be devoted to prisons, the most at-risk institution for hauntings and possessions. Little wonder that they have failed so miserably at rehabilitation and that recidivism rates are so high. Could they be made more safe and humane and effective for all concerned— inmates, staff, and visitors—by psychopomps?

Could psychopomps offer counseling and support group services, via the internet and other means, to near-death experiencers to help them understand and heal their discomfort? Not only do the experiencers find it hard to share their trauma with others, but their isolation has been linked to adverse mental health effects. Sharing gives them relief from fear, confusion, embarrassment, denial, and dissociation. Since they often undergo psychic and related life changes, including involvement in shamanic practice, they can benefit greatly from the mentoring of qualified shaman-psychopomps.

Finally, people still alive but medically "dead to the world" might benefit. Psychopomp skills should be easily transferable to serve those suffering from coma, dementia, concussion, botched anesthesia, anaphylactic shock, amnesia, feverish delirium, drug overdose, stroke, and other situations of compromised consciousness. True, persons depend on the brain for normal functioning in ordinary reality, but not for their existence. The self is not impaired, the brain is. Persons simply cannot express themselves in the usual way, so they need an unusual—a nonordinary—way, namely a shamanic one.

Such service too may help prevent nocebo misdiagnoses of patients, whose intent to stay alive and return to normal life may still be strong and clear to the shaman. Finding this out may be especially comforting to families who have given up hope for the misdiagnosed "terminally ill." Might ambulance crews and other emergency workers be schooled in the possibility and even necessity of communicating with the "departed"? For that and more, stay tuned.

JonBenet 3. The three students who got the big hits floored us all: (7) large city; man-made structure; posters; cluttered; sadness; fear; urgency; messy; tired; small objects; child's room; stuffed animals; flashing police lights; maybe child missing; kidnapping; blond victim; (8) man-made structure; basement; mountains; cool; damp; house with chimney and peaked roofs;

dead body; pitiful; sad; angry; something is hidden here; (9) huge mountains; brick house with chimney; haunted; peaceful neighborhood but a mystery has risen from this place; Colorado; very cold; snow; ice; icicles; footprints; wet; slippery; terror; fear inside; mystery; negative questions; kidnapping; murder; December 26, 1994; 7 year-old blonde victim. Student 8 drew a sketch closely resembling the house, and student 9 drew a nearly perfect one. Was JonBenet speaking to us from the beyond? You decide.

APPENDIX

Mythic Allies

The listing below offers an expedient sample of mythological gods and goddesses of major cultures dealing in some way with departing and departed souls. Such samples have long been used in research, their value depending on the breadth of coverage and on the number and diversity of cases. In no way is it meant to be complete or perfectly representative, but instead is presented simply to reference the many death-related spirits of many traditions, as well as to illustrate the typical themes and symbols of classic psychopomp practice, across the world throughout the ages.

Europe

Across the European region, Pagans, Muslims, Christians, and Jews all revere Michael the Archangel, who guards souls on their afterlife journey. Russian lore depicts him as a ferryman taking souls to paradise. Gabriel the Archangel also escorts the dead to the beyond.

The European King of Terrors, related to the Grim Reaper, is depicted driving dead souls before him.

The Greek ferryman spirit Charon, sometimes depicted with wolf ears, used Styx, the Goddess of the

River, to help departed souls cross from earth to the underworld.

The Greek 3-headed dog-god Cerberus guards the portal to the afterlife by preventing the dead from escaping and the living from entering.

The Greek goddess Hekate, Queen of Ghosts, who may manifest with wings or as a dog or with dogs, rules passages between life and death.

The winged Greek god Hermes conveys souls of the dead to Hades.

The Greek goddess Iris guides female souls over a rainbow bridge to the Realm of the Dead.

The winged Greek spirits, the Erotes, guide souls to the next realm.

Greek bird-women spirits escort souls, in particular unlucky seafarers, to Persephone, Queen of the Dead, sometimes appearing and singing to them before death.

The Greek god Thanatos brings death to people then escorts them to their new home.

The Russian bird-woman goddess Sirin serenades the dying to lead them joyfully into the realm of the dead.

The Bavarian goddess Berchta in the realm of the dead cares for souls who died as babies, were driven to suicide by broken hearts or despair, were not given a proper burial, or lack living people to remember them. She also helps escort troublesome discarnate souls to a state of peace.

The Dutch goddess Hulda receives the souls of the newly dead into her realm.

The Irish Banshee, Welsh Cyhyraeth, and Scottish Caointeach spirits wail before deaths and then escort the dead souls to the Other Side. The Irish Banshee may serve as a family's personal escort to the realm of the dead.

The Celtic male spirit Manannan Mac Lir ferries discarnate souls from the earth realm across to Mag Mell, his Otherworld Realm.

The Celtic goddess Morgan Le Fay, whose bird is a crow and whose name derived from the words for sea and mermaid, serves humans as a psychopomp.

The Celtic goddess Epona may also have served as a psychopomp.

In Brittany the god Ankou delivers discarnate souls to a ferryman who transfers them to the Isle of the West.

The Welsh Hounds of Annwn belonging to Arawn escorted, protected, and guided dead souls to the Otherworld.

The Irish goddess Aynia leads those souls she loves and admires to the Other Side.

The Etruscan god Charun collects discarnate souls and escorts them to the afterlife.

The Etruscan goddess Vanth, sometimes appearing with wings, escorts dead souls to their next destination.

The Etruscan god Turms, with winged shoes, guides the dead.

Many of the Swan Goddesses of Northern Europe serve as psychopomps traveling between the realms of life and death.

The Norse Valkyries, goddesses of life and death manifesting as ravens and swans and sometimes riding wolves, guide souls to the next realm. They escort fallen warriors to Odin's hall, Valhalla, where they serve as hostesses.

The Norse and Germanic god Odin, accompanied by wolves and ravens, communicates with departed souls and serves deceased warriors in his hall. He is said to morph into a bird to fly around the land of the dead.

The Norse goddess Hel is keeper of departed souls in the Realm of the Dead, which she rules.

The Germanic goddess Frau Gaude serves as a psychopomp.

The German goddess Frau Wacholder opens and closes the portal between the living and dead.

The Balkan goddess Samovila, who manifests as a swan woman, leads human souls to their next home.

The Macedonian goddesses of thresholds, the Samovili, who may manifest as winged women, provide escort service for the dead.

The Finno-Ugric World Surveyor Man, in the form of a swan or crane, guides the dead to their next life.

The Finnish goddess Tuonetar, Queen of the Realm of the Dead, escorts souls across Manala, the river separating life and death.

The Lithuanian goddess Veliona, Guardian of Water, protects the dead and personally receives fallen warriors into her realm.

Middle East

The Sumerian goddess Ereshkigal meets, controls, and commands the newly dead.

The Egyptian god Anubis, who manifests with the head of a black jackal or hound, guides departed souls and presides over the hall of judgment.

The Egyptian goddess Heket is a guardian of the dead.

The Egyptian god Wepwawet opens the road for new souls to go to the womb and for dead ones to come to the afterlife.

The Egyptian god Shu, portrayed wearing ostrich feathers, was believed to hold the ladder that the deceased used to climb to heaven.

The Iranian goddess Anahita, who in the form of a vulture helps the shaman-psychopomp, guides souls on their postmortem voyage.

The Iranian god Vayu helps the departed cross a bridge to the Other Side. In some accounts the soul sees a beautiful girl with two dogs near the bridge.

Muslims say that Gabriel the Archangel escorted Muhammed on his heavenly journey.

The Judaic female spirit Shekhina may serve human souls as a psychopomp.

Asia

Hawaiian Night Marcher spirits serve as psychopomps who protect and escort newly deceased souls on their journey to the beyond.

The Tantric goddess Vajravetali guards the threshold between living and dying, banishing our fear of death and the afterlife.

The Indian god Agni guides souls to non-earthly realms.

The ancient Indian god Yama, Lord of Death, lassoes the departed soul to bring it into his realm. The soul is advised not to be intimidated by his four-eyed dogs during its trip in a boat on a river.

The Indian god Indra serves deceased warriors in his hall.

The Indian goddess Marichi protects discarnate souls against vicious spirits.

The Indian goddess Kamakhya banishes malevolent ghosts.

The Vietnamese goddesses Lady Tung and Lady Tai preside over the threshold between the realms of life and death.

The Japanese god Enma determines the next destination of a departed soul, depending of the virtue of the person's life.

The Japanese god Jizo guards dead souls, especially those of aborted, miscarried, and stillborn children.

The Japanese god Wanyudo patrols the border between life and death, ferrying dead souls to the netherworld.

The Chinese goddess Ma Zu rescues sailors at sea during storms and comforts restive ghosts after disastrous sea tragedies like tsunamis in order to cleanse and clear the locale.

The Chinese goddess Hsi Wang Mu is a guardian of the dead.

The Thai female spirit Mae Thoranee vanquishes malevolent spirits.

The Korean goddess Pali Kongju soothes stuck and restless ghosts and rescues them by leading them over the threshold of death.

The Korean goddess Abandoned Princess leads souls through their death process to the "good place."

In Korea, the male Emissary Spirit from the World of Darkness takes part in a shamanic ceremony to guide the departed soul on its walk into the afterlife.

The Tibetan goddess Tara, whose name derives from the Sanskrit "to cross over," brings dangerous ghosts to enlightenment so they can become protectors of humans.

In the Tibetan region, the Na-Khi spirit Dto-mba Shila is imitated and invoked by shamans before conducting souls into the afterlife.

Among the Malaysian Semai, the spirits Munkar and Nangkir return the souls of the dead to the other world.

The Indonesian Taman goddess Grandmother Siunsun Amas guides souls to the land of the dead.

Africa and the Caribbean

The Dahomean and Haitian Vodou god Agwe, King of the Sea and husband of the mermaid Sirene, protects seafarers and leads dead souls to the realm of the dead, which is beneath the sea. Sirene is sometimes depicted in the presence of a boat, her ceremonial symbol.

The Yoruba goddess Olokun controls the passageway through which souls must transit between life and afterlife.

The Yoruba goddess Oya calms deceased souls and so prevents hauntings. She helps shamans by responding to banners woven in nine distinct colors.

The Congolese water snake god Simbi controls water channels, including that separating the realms of living and dead, sometimes serving as a psychopomp for departed souls, especially those of shamans.

Vodou practitioners have provided psychopomp service in the Cities of the Dead locale in New Orleans with the help of their spirit allies. Marie Laveau the First, famous C19th shaman in New Orleans, served as a psychopomp for executed prisoners. One of her helping spirits was the Virgin Mary.

The Americas

The Mesoamerican man-dog spirit Xolotl leads souls on their journey to the realm of death.

The Aztec female spirit Mictlancihuatl and the male spirit Mictlantecuhtli guard and preside over souls in the afterlife.

The Mexican goddess La Santissima Muerte can banish ghosts.

The Mexican god Tlaloc, Lord of Rain, receives souls who died from drowning and lightning strikes.

The Zapotec goddess Itzpapalotl presides over a paradise realm for the souls of stillborn children and women who died in childbirth.

The Maya goddess Ix Tab escorts souls to the afterlife.

The Puerto Rican goddess La Madama banishes troublesome ghosts.

In North American traditions, Crow/Raven travel back and forth between the lands of the living and the dead.

According to the Ojibwe, Crow accompanies the dead to the Other Side.

The Kwakiutl god Bukwas leads souls to transit into the Realm of the Dead.

The Inuit goddess Pinga escorts the dead to a transit area where their souls are purified before moving to a more pleasant realm.

CHAPTER ENDNOTES

Introduction

Ishi: Rogers, 2009:63

Near-death experiencers return: Kowalewski, 2014; Neimark, 2003; Sutherland, 1989

Communicate with ghosts: Lawrence, 2015:7

Core shamanic practice since ancient times: Illes, 2009:853; Lepp, 2004:217; Overton, 2000

Latter souls: Kowalewski & de la Iglesia, 2014

Literature exceptions: Fiore, 1995; Madden, 1999; Rain, 1989

Few books on psychopomps: Fritz, 2003; Sullivan, 2012; Sullivan & Sullivan, 2013; Winkowski, 2011

Large gatherings of shamans: Omega Institute, 2002, 2003

Ken Ring: 2006

Jesus as shaman: Craffert, 2008; Jackie Jones-Hunt, 2011

Interest in the paranormal: Leary, 2012; Vyse, 1997; Walker, 2009

Psychopomp service for the departed: Carson, 2013b

Requires a healthy psyche: Noory & Guiley, 2011

Chapter

1 Dead Men Talking

Two-thirds of Americans: Greeley, 1987

Telepathy: Butler & Butler, 2014; Myers, 2005:28; Sheldrake & Lambert, 2007

Recent articles and books: Beichler 2007; Benor, 1992; Charbonier, Jean, 2015; Ostrander and Schroeder 1997; Radin 1997, 2006, 2013; Sounds True, 2008; Tart 2009; Utts, 1996

Deceased loved ones: White, 2012

Electrifying vibrations: Hering, 2008:49; Stevenson, 1992

Appear to relatives in dreams: Balzano, 2008:13

Large majority of Americans: harrisinteractive.com; Long & Perry, 2010; religions.pewforum.org

2009 and 2007 surveys: religions.pewforum.org; Heathcote-James, 2011; Wicker, 2009:4-5

Century of evidence: Carter, 2012b; Laszlo & Peake, 2014

Recent scientific research: Almeder, 1992; Long and Perry, 2010

Gone native: Goodman, 1997; Green, 2007; M. Harner, 2013; E. Turner, 1992;

Comprehensive reviews: Fontana, 2005; Lester, 2005; Peake, 2009

Surveys show: Eaton, 2011; Editorial, 2010; LaGrand, 2006; Wright, 1998, 2008

Certain "classic" happenings: Noory & Guiley, 2011

Phone calls: Arcangel, 2005; Bayliss & Rogo, 1955; Carter, 2012b; Lindstrom, 1995; Robertson, 2013; Varga, 2009

Studies have reported: Batey, 1980; Osis, 1979; Wright, 2004

Cross-correspondences: Carter, 2012b; Keen, 2003; Laszlo & Peake, 2014; Wilson, 2011

Meta-analyses: Stevenson, 1992; Tart, 2009

Studies of remote-viewing: Schnabel, 1997

Evidence from near-death experiences: Green, 1998, 2001, 2008; Ring, 2006; van Lommel, 2011

Despite efforts: Neimark, 2003

Studies show: Long & Perry, 2010

Distinguishing features: Overton, 2000:38

Global study: Rosenblatt et al., 1976

Native-Americans: M. Harner, 2009

2003 and 2005 polls: harrisinteractive.com; religioustolerance.org; Higgins & Bergman, 2011:194

Hauntings: Batey, 1980; Schwalm, 1995; Stevenson, 1995; Wickham, 2011

Instrumental transcommunication: Ellis, 2011; Konstantinos, 2004; Noory & Guiley, 2011

Quantitative investigations: Fenwick & Fenwick, 2008; Hart, 1956; Houran, 2002; Schmeidler, 1966

Sheep and goats: Maher & Hansen, 1995

Professional counselors: Hogan, 2014; Tick, 2013

Core skills: M. Harner, 2010; Harner & Harner, 2000; Hering, 2008; Jensen, 2001; Robinson, 1998

Figurines: Goodman, 1990, 1997; Gore, 1995

Recent studies: M. Harner, 2003; S. Harner, 2003; Vuckovic et al., 2007; clinicaltrials.gov/ct2/show/nct00071474

Research too: Carter, 2012b

Respected clinicians: Fiore, 1995

Multiple personality: Betty, 2012

Little power to affect: Wickham, 2011

Soul will not believe: Rain, 1989

Near-death experience skills: Green, 1998a, 2001; Groth-Marnat & Summers, 1998; M. Harner, 2013; Jilek, 1971; Long & Perry, 2010; Roberts & Owen, 1988; Sartori, 2014; Stout et al., 2006; Sutherland, 1989

2 Who? Where? When?

Vehicle and industrial accidents: Wickham, 2011

Katrina: Filan, 2007

Battlefields: Carter, 2012b

Suicides: Moss, 2006b

Resentful: Dulam, 2004

Ethnocentric spirits: M. Harner, 2009

Spirit thieves: Ingerman, 2001

Survivors cling: Gore, 1995

Violent death sites: Ingerman & Stevens, 2011; Brunton, 2001

Clinics: Fiore, 1995

Anesthesia: Sagan, 1997

Old hotels: Higgins & Bergman, 2011

Burial site: Eaton, 2011:86

Emotional significance: Guggenheim & Guggenheim, 1995; Higgins & Bergman, 2011

Visitation dreams: Eaton, 2011; Guggenheim & Guggenheim, 1995; M. Harner, 2009; Heathcote-James, 2011

Emotional arousal: Jensen, 2001

3 Who Benefits?

Simply lost: Harner & Harner, 2000

Deaths of spouses: Selye, 1978

Hungry ghosts: Holt, 2004:774

Vagabond souls: Wilcox, 2004:166

Navajo: Laughlin, 2004

Washo: Handelman, 1967

Boniwa: Conklin, 2004

Sensing ghosts: Peters, 2010

Study of widows: Lindstrom, 1995

Positive health: Murray & Pizzorno, 1998

Last goodbyes: Kenin-Lopsan, 2013

Proper last rites: Tick, 2007

Disturbed discarnate souls: Boykova, 2004; Eliade, 1992; Marriat, 2006

Selfish or harmful intent: Knecht, 2004

Reports of hauntings: Betty, 2015; Ellis, 2011; Reader's Digest, 2008.

Physical maladies: Sifers, 2003

Attacks: Hamayon, 2004

Psychological sufferings: Achterberg, 1985; Anderson et al., 1994; Balch, 2002; Bower, 1991; Dein, 2012; Hammerschlag, 1994; Kyle, 1993; Lee, 2010; Murphy & Pizzorno, 1998; Solomon, 1990

Very young: Emmons, 2001

A discarnate soul: Cumes, 2013

Alcohol: Fiore, 1995; Moss, 2006a

Possessor: Craig, 1988

Therapy: Craig, 1988

Near-death experiencers often find it hard: Eaton, 2011; Groth-Marnat & Summers, 1998; Long & Perry, 2010; Ring, 1989; Rominger, 2009; Stout et al., 2006

Shaman's task: Lepp, 2004:217

Highways: Larramendi, 2010; Wickham, 2011

Police: Higgins & Bergman, 2011

4 What Psychopomps Do

Discarnate thieves: Kowalewski, 2012a

Halfway house: Eaton, 2011:25

Initiated by the near-death experience: Green, 2001; M. Harner, 2013; Jilek, 1971; Kowalewski, 2014; Morse & Perry, 1992; Neimark, 2003; Noll, 1985; Roberts & Owen, 1988; Sutherland, 1989

Communicates telepathically: Kowalewski, 2011, 2012b

Analogous to the near-death experience: Walsh, 1989

Oldest spiritual practices: M. Harner 1997, 2010; Harner & Harner, 2000; Hering, 2008; Jensen, 2001; Robinson, 1998

Important one in all shamanic cultures: Noll, 2004:237; Pratt, 2007; Wood, 2015

Jesus: 1 Peter 4:6

Shamans do not work alone: Bergstrom, 2011

Disaster sites: Ingerman & Stevens, 2011

Meet other spirits: Gore, 1998

Energy body: Brennan, 1993; Carter, 2012b:294-298; Higgins & Bergman, 2011; Oschman, 2000; Taylor, 2009, 2014; Villoldo, 1998; von Braschler, 2012

Decline effect: Butler, 1978; Radin, 2006

Anything magical: Carter, 2012b; Wilson, 2008

Fantasy prone: Noll, 1985

Field effects: Citro, 2011:151, 199

Experienced meditators: Radin et al., 2012; Radin, 2013

Linde: 2004:451

Shapes matter: Radin, 2013:314, 317, original emphasis

Key tools: Tart, 2009

Neither time nor space: Guggenheim & Guggenheim, 1995:252

Telepathy and clairvoyance: Tart, 2009

Full of meaning: Geske, 1997

Various reasons people get stuck: Moen, 2014:84.

Literature and popular lore: Peters, 2010

Despair: Geske, 1997

5 Mythic Resources

Vision quest: M. Harner, 2013

Specialist spirits: Gignoux, 2004

After shamans die: M. Harner, 1995

Probably a large number: Eliade, 1992:310, 388; Campbell, 1990

Took great care to recount: M. Harner, 2004

Korea: Kister, 2004:686

Brazil: Conklin, 2004

Listing: Eliade, 1992; Illes, 2009; Walter & Fridman, 2004

The only caveat: Sluten, 2015

Theme of moving water: Chi-Bikom, 2004; Eliade, 1992; McCall, 2004

Funerary bridge: Eliade, 1992:482

Boat and ferryman: Eliade, 1992; Emeagwali & Walter, 2004; Ephirin-Donkor, 2004; Kister, 2004; Lepp, 2004; Rysdyk, 2015; Taylor, 2009; Winzeler, 2004

Therianthropes: Lewis-Williams & Dowson, 1988

Canines: Eliade, 1992

Esoteric lore: Carter, 2012b; Guggenheim & Guggenheim, 1995; Wilson, 2008

Scientific studies: Sheldrake, 2011

The ability to turn into a bird: Eliade, 1992:343, 403
Taoist: Eliade, 1992
Buryat: K. Turner, 2013
Birds are psychopomps: Eliade, 1992:95
Bird features: Walsh, 2007
China: Moss, 2006b
Yokut: Eliade, 1992
Mongolians: Boykova & Walter, 2004:558
Ravens: King, 2013; see also Turk, 2009
Birds: Eliade, 1992
Finno-Ugrians: Corradi-Musi, 2004
Studies of afterlife communications: Higgins & Bergman, 2011:200
Wildlife biologists: Steinhart, 1995.

6 Trip Planner

Best advice: T. Cowan, 1996; Guggenheim & Guggenheim, 1995; Robinson, 1998
Academic experience: Kowalewski, 2003
Their cases select them: Higgins, 2014
Good advance work: Kowalewski, 2012b
Full of power: T. Cowan, 2011
Distraught emotional state: Eliade, 1992
Sonic driving: Maxfield, 1994
Body postures: Goodman, 1990; Gore, 1995
The unexpected: Kowalewski, 2011
Tibetan: Wangyal, 2004
Analytical overlay: Radin, 2013:186
Asking questions: Ingerman, 2001; Jensen, 2001
Psychotherapy for the dead: M. Harner, 2009; see also Green, 2015; Silvana, 2009
Turn malevolent spirits around: Gorshunova, 2004

Ways of escorting: Moss, 2006b

Group transitions: Bryan, 2013; Eliade, 1992; Ingerman & Stevens, 2011; Peters, 2010

7 Strategies

Trickery as a ploy: Peters, 1981

Shots of brandy: Eliade, 1992

Family reunion at home: Jensen, 2001

Having a parent appear: Paasche, 2013

Ancient shamanic accounts: Eliade, 1992

Nefarious spirits: King, 2013

Harner tells the story: 2009

Just because you're dead: Kübler-Ross, 1991

8 Patterns

Variety of feelings: Rain, 1989

Failure to forgive: Moss, 2006b

Deceased Inuit shamans: Tein et al., 1994

Soul's love and respect: E. Cowan, 1992; Moss, 2006b

Psychopomp story: Geske, 1997

Near-death experiencers too encounter: Long & Perry, 2010

Children are especially sensitive: Guggenheim & Guggenseim, 1995; Higgins & Bergman, 2011

Up to one-half of college students: Jaynes, 1986; see also Geiger, 2013

Crying Way: M. Harner, 1995

Never trust a shaman: Brown, 2007

Tibetan psychopomps: Berglie, 2004

Unique color schemes: Butler, 1978

Palliative carers: Taylor, 2014

Dressed as light: Espinoza, 1995:7

Symbol research: Kowalewski, 1980
Teams: Laszlo & Peake, 2014:82
Obsessive disorder: Illes, 2009

9 Real or Make-Believe?

Truth-seeking skeptics: Kowalewski, 2004, 2012
Micmac: Berggren, 1998:xi
Alphanumerics: Higgins & Bergman, 2011
Surviving guests: Woolley, 2010
Three more scenarios: Carter, 2012b; Myers, 2005
Bathed in such a light: Guggenheim & Guggenheim, 1995
Chukchi: Howard, 2002:61

10 What the Dead Can Teach the Living

Feel a heaviness: Eaton, 2011
Andean shaman: Espinoza, 1995:7, 85
Ancient shaman: Eliade, 1992
Hospice care: Bryan, 2013
Big data: Smith, 2015
Safer health measures: Starfield, 2000
Democide: Rummel, 1997
Cases of possession: M. Harner, 2009
Already some coroners: Carson, 2013b
Near-death experiencers find it hard: Palmer & Broad, 2002; Pennebaher, 1999; Roberts & Owen, 1988; Rominger, 2009
Psychopomp skills: Madden, 1999; Tunney, 2013
Persons depend on the brain: Betty, 2014

Appendix: Mythic Allies

Expedient sample: Gurr, 1972

REFERENCES

Achterberg, Jeanne. 1985. *Imagery in Healing.* New York, NY: New Science Library.

Almeder, Robert. 1992. *Death and Personal Survival: The Evidence for Life after Death.* New York, NY: Rowman & Littlefield.

Anderson, Barbara, Janice Kiecolt-Glaser, & Ronald Glaser. 1994. "A Biobehavioral Model of Cancer Stress and Disease Course." *American Psychologist* 49, 5 (May):389-404.

Andrews, Ted. 1996. *Animal-Speak: The Spiritual and Magical Powers of Creatures Great and Small.* St. Paul, MN: Llewellyn.

Arcangel, Dianne. 2005. *Afterlife Encounters.* Newburyport, MA: Hampton Roads.

Balch, Phyllis. 2002. *Prescription for Herbal Healing.* New York, NY: Penguin Putnam.

Balzano, Christopher. 2008. *Ghostly Adventures.* Avon, MA: Adams Media.

Batey, Boyce. 1980. "Evidence for Life after Death." *Journal of Religion and Psychical Research* 3, 1 (January):47-51.

Bayliss, R., & D. Rogo. 1955. *Phone Calls from the Dead*. New York, NY: Berkeley.

Becker, Robert, & Gary Selden. 1985. *Body Electric*. New York, NY: William Morrow.

Beichler, James. 2007. "Trend or Trendy? The Development and Acceptance of the Paranormal by the Scientific Community." *Journal of Spirituality and Paranormal Studies* 30, 1 (January):41-57.

Benor, Daniel. 1992. *Healing Research*. Oxfordshire, UK: Helix.

Berggren, Karen. 1998. *Circle of Shaman*. Rochester, VT: Destiny.

Berglie, Per-Arne. 2004. "Tibetan Shamanism." Pp. 790-798 in Walter & Fridman.

Bergstrom, B. 2011. "Protection and Allies in Heart-Centered Shamanic Healing: An Interview with Christina Pratt." *Journal of Shamanic Practice,* 4, 1 (Spring):19-24.

Betty, Stafford. 2012. "Growing Evidence for Demonic Possession." *Journal of Spirituality and Paranormal Studies* 35, 1 (January):23-40.

_____. 2014. Review of Chris Carter's *Science and the Afterlife Experience. Journal for Spiritual and Consciousness Studies* 37, 3 (July):171-175.

_____. 2015. "Growing Evidence for 'Demonic Possession': Lessons for Psychiatry." *Journal for Spirituality and Consciousness Studies* 38, 1 (May):36-60.

Bower, Bruce. 1991. "Questions of Mind over Immunity." *Science News* 139 (6 April):216-217.

Boykova, Elena. 2004. "Funeral Rites in Eurasian Shamanism." Pp. 557-564 in Walter & Fridman.

Braschler, Von. 2012. *Seven Secrets of Time Travel: Mystic Voyages of the Energy Body*. Rochester, VT: Destiny.

Brennan, Barbara. 1993. *Light Emerging: The Journey of Personal Healing*. New York, NY: Bantam.

Brown, Tom, Jr. 2007. Way of the Shaman. Workshop, Tracker School, St. Petersburg, FL.

Brunton, Bill. 2001. "Healing the Aftermath of Terror." *Shamanism* 14, 2 (Fall-Winter):5.

Bryan, Leslie. 2013. "A Shamanic Presence in Hospice Care." Pp. 181-194 in Carson.

Butler, Tom, & Lisa Butler. 2014. "Media Watch." *Searchlight: Newsletter of the Academy for Spiritual and Consciousness Studies* 23, 4 (December):6-7.

Butler, W.E. 1978. *How to Read the Aura and Practice Psychometry, Telepathy, & Clairvoyance*. Rochester, VT: Destiny.

Campbell, Joseph. 1990. *Primitive Mythology*. New York, NY: Viking.

Carson, Cecile (ed.). 2013a. *Spirited Medicine: Shamanism in Contemporary Healthcare*. Baltimore, MD: Otter Bay.

_____. 2013b. "Introduction." Pp. xv-xxi in Carson.

Carter, Chris. 2012a. *Science and Psychic Phenomena: The Fall of the House of Skeptics*. Rochester, VT: Inner Traditions.

_____. 2012b. *Science and the Afterlife Experience: Evidence for the Immortality of Consciousness*. Rochester, VT: Inner Traditions.

Charbonier, Jean. 2015. *Seven Reasons to Believe in the Afterlife: A Doctor Reviews the Case for Consciousness after Death*. Rochester, VT: Inner Traditions.

Chi-bikom, Ismael. 2004. "Cape Nguni Shamanism." Pp. 914-920 in Walter & Fridman.

Conklin, Beth. 2004. "Amazon Funeral Rites and Shamanism (Brazil)." Pp. 375-378 in Walter & Fridman.

Corradi-Musi, Carla. 2004. "Finno-Ugric Shamanism." Pp. 486-496 in Walter & Fridman.

Cowan, Eliot. 1992. "Interview with an Irish Shaman." *Shamanism* 5, 1 (Summer):4-19.

Cowan, Tom. 1996. *Shamanism as a Spiritual Practice for Daily Life*. Langhorne, PA: Crossing Press.

_____. 2011. "Moments of Grace and Transformation: Tending Joplin, Missouri." *Journal of Shamanic Practice* 4, 2 (Fall):36-40.

Craffert, Pieter. 2008. *Life of a Galilean Shaman*. Eugene, OR: Cascade.

Craig, Wesley. 1988. "The Dark Side: Dealing with Evil Spirits in Hypno-Therapeutic Sessions." *Journal of Religion and Psychical Research* 11, 1 (January):14-26.

Cumes, David. 2013. "South African Indigenous Healing." Pp. 197-216 in Carson.

Dein, Simon. 2012. "Mental Health and the Paranormal." *International Journal of Transpersonal Studies* 31, 1:61-74.

Dulam, Sendenjav. 2004. "Spirits and Ghosts in Mongolia." Pp. 627-629 in Walter & Fridman.

Eaton, B. 2011. *Afterlife*. New York, NY: Penguin.

Editorial. 2010. "New Age Americans." *Noetic Post* 1, 2 (Spring-Summer):12.

Eliade, Mircea. 1992. *Shamanism: Archaic Techniques of Ecstasy.* Princeton, NJ: Princeton University Press.

Ellis, Mellissa. 2011. *101 Ways to Find a Ghost*. Avon, MA: Adams Media.

Emeagwali, Gloria, & Mariko Walter. 2004. "Ancient Egyptian Shamanism." Pp. 906-910 in Walter & Fridman.

Emmons, C. 2001. "On Being a Medium in a 'Rational Society'." *Anthropology of Consciousness,* 12 (1), 71-82.

Ephirim-Donkor, Anthony. 2004. "Ancestor Worship in Africa." Pp. 899-906 in Walter & Fridman.

Espinoza, Luis. 1995. *Chamalú: The Shamanic Way of the Heart.* Rochester, VT: Destiny.

Fenwick, Peter, & Elizabeth Fenwick. 2008. *Art of Dying: A Journey to Elsewhere.* New York, NY: Bloomsbury Academics.

Filan, Kenaz. 2007. *Haitian Vodou Handbook.* Rochester, VT: Destiny.

Fiore, Edith. 1995. *Unquiet Dead.* New York, NY: Ballantine.

Fontana, David. 2005. *Is There an Afterlife?* Blue Ridge Summit, PA: O Books.

Foster, R., G. Bradish, Y. Dobyns, B. Dunne, & R. Jahn. 1996. "Field REG Anomalies in Group Situations." *Journal of Scientific Exploration* 10, 1:111-141.

_____. 1998. "Field REG II—Consciousness Field Effects: Replications and Explorations." *Journal of Scientific Exploration* 12, 3:425-454.

Fritz, F.J. 2003. *Shamanic Psychopomp.* Bloomington, IN: 1st Books Library.

Fugh-Berman, Adriane. 1996. *Alternative Medicine: What Works?* Berkeley, CA: Odonian.

Geiger, John. 2013. *Angel Effect.* Philadelphia, PA: Weinstein.

Geske, Steve. 1997. "Healing Death for the Living." *Shamanism* 10. 2 (Fall-Winter). shamanism.org.

Gignoux, Philippe. 2004. "Ancient Iranian Religions and Shamanism." Pp. 529-532 in Walter & Fridman.

Goodman, Felicitas. 1990. *Where the Spirits Ride the Wind: Trance Journeys and Other Ecstatic Experiences.* Bloomington, IN: Indiana University Press.

_____. 1997. Ecstatic Postures. Workshop, Omega Institute, Rhinebeck, NY.

Gore, Belinda. 1995. *Ecstatic Body Postures.* Santa Fe, NM: Bear.

Gorshunova, Olga. "Tajik Shamanism." Pp. 629-632 in Walter & Fridman.

Greeley, A. 1987. "Mysticism Goes Mainstream." *American Health* 6, 1:47-49.

Green, J. Timothy. 1998a. "Near-Death Experiences." *Shamanism* 11, 2 (Fall-Winter):shamanism.org.

_____. 1998b. "Near Death Experiences, Shamanism, and the Scientific Method." *Journal of Near-Death Studies* 16, 3 (Spring):205-222.

_____. 2001. "The Near-Death Experience as a Shamanic Initiation." *Shamanism* 14, 2 (Fall-Winter):13-23.

_____. 2007. "Death Journey of a Hopi Indian." *Shamanism* 20, 2 (Fall-Winter):40-45.

_____. 2008. "Death Journey." *Shamanism* 20, 8 (Fall-Winter): shamanism.org.

Green, Veche. 2015. "Soaring of the Great Garuda." *Sacred Hoop* 88:34-37.

Groth-Marnat, G., & R. Summers. 1998. "Altered Beliefs, Attitudes, and Behaviors Following Near-Death Experiences." *Journal of Humanistic Psychology* 38, 3 (Summer):110-125.

Gruning, Herb. 1998. "The Spirit of Jesus as a Haunting Phenomenon." *Journal of Religion and Psychical Research* 21, 1 (January):50-52.

Guggenheim, B., & J. Guggenheim. 1995. *Hello from Heaven: A New Field of Research—After-Death Communication—Confirms That Life and Love Are Eternal.* New York, NY: Bantam.

Gurr, Ted Robert. 1972. *Polimetrics.* Englewood Cliffs, NJ: Prentice-Hall.

Hamayon, Roberte. 2004. "Siberian Shamanism." Pp. 618-627 in Walter & Fridman.

Hammerschlag, Carl. 1994. *Theft of the Spirit.* New York, NY: Simon & Schuster.

Handelman, Don. 1967. "Development of a Washo Shaman." *Ethnology* 6, 4 (October):444-464.

Harner, Michael. 1990. *Way of the Shaman.* San Francisco, CA: HarperCollins.

_____. 1995. Basic Workshop. Foundation for Shamanic Studies, Omega Institute, Rhinebeck, NY.

_____. 1997. "Shamanic Healing: We Are Not Alone." *Shamanism* 10, 1 (Spring-Summer):4-7.

_____. 2003. "Foundation Letter." Foundation for Shamanic Studies, Mill Valley, CA.

_____. 2004. "Shamanism, Myth, and Reality." Audio talk, Foundation for Shamanic Studies, Mill Valley, CA. shamanism.org.

_____. 2009. Three-Year Program in Advanced Shamanic Initiation, Foundation for Shamanic Studies. Institute of Noetic Sciences, Petaluma, CA.

_____. 2010. *Michael Harner Audio Talks.* Foundation for Shamanic Studies, Mill Valley, CA. shamanism.org.

_____. 2013. *Cave and Cosmos: Shamanic Encounters with Another Reality.* Berkeley, CA: North Atlantic Books.

_____, & Sandra Harner. 2000. "Core Practices in the Shamanic Treatment of Illness." *Shamanism* 13, 1-2 (Fall-Winter):19-30.

Harner, Sandra. 2003. "Shamanic Journeying and Immune Response: Hypothesis Testing." *Shamanism* 16, 2 (Fall-Winter):9-14.

_____. 2010. "Shamanic Journeying and Immune Response: Hypothesis Testing." *Shamanism Annual* 23:31-34.

Hart, Hornell. 1956. "Six Theories about Apparitions." *Proceedings of the Society for Psychical Research* 50, 185 (May):153-239.

Heathcote-James, E. 2011. *After-Death Communication.* London, UK: John Blake.

Hering, Elynne. 2008. "Psychopomp Summons." *Shamanism* 20, 2 (Fall-Winter):47-49.

Higgins, Joe. 2014. "Receiving and Understanding Signs." Pp. 161-170 in Hogan.

_____, & C. Bergman. 2011. *Everything Guide to Evidence of the Afterlife: A Scientific Approach to Proving the Existence of Life after Death.* Avon, MA: Adams Media.

Hogan, R. (ed.). 2014. *New Developments in Afterlife Communication.* Loxahatchie, FL: Academy for Spiritual and Consciousness Studies.

Holt, John. 2004. "Priestesses (Mediums) of Sri Lanka." Pp. 773-775 in Walter & Fridman.

Houran, James. 2002. "Analysis of Haunting Experiences at a Historical Illinois Landmark." *Australian Journal of Parapsychology* 2, 2:97-124.

Howard, K. 2002. "Shaman Music, Drumming, and into the 'New Age'." *Shaman* 10, 2:59-81.

Illes, J. 2009. *Encyclopedia of Spirits.* New York, NY: HarperOne.

Ingerman, Sandra. 2001. Two-Week Program in Shamanic Healing, Foundation for Shamanic Studies. Sunrise Springs Retreat Center, Albuquerque, NM.

_____, & Jose Stevens. 2011. "Historical Perspectives." Pp. 5-7 in Society for Shamanic Practitioners (ed.), *Shamanism without Borders.* Olivenhain, CA. SSP.

Institute of Noetic Sciences. 2008. "Spirituality Poll." *Shift Report.* Petaluma, CA: IONS.

Jaynes, Julian. 1986. "Consciousness and the Voice of the Mind." *Canadian Psychology* 27, 2 (April):169-173.

Jensen, Sharon. 2001. "Psychopomp Work at the World Trade Center." *Shamanism* 14, 2 (Fall-Winter):64-65.

Jilek, Wolfgang. 1971. "From Crazy Witch Doctor to Auxiliary Psychotherapist—the Changing Image of the Medicine Man." *Psychiatria Clinica* 4:200-220.

_____. 1982. "Altered States of Consciousness in North-American Ceremonials." *Ethos* 10, 4 (Winter):326-343.

Jones-Hunt, Jackie. 2011. *Moses and Jesus: The Shamans.* Blue Ridge Summit, PA: Moon Books.

Kalweit, Holger. 1988. *Dreamtime and Inner Space.* Boston, MA: Shambhala.

Keen, Montague. 2003. "Communicating with the Dead: The Evidence Ignored Why Paul Kortus Is Wrong." *Journal of Scientific Exploration* 17, 2:291-299.

Kenin-Lopsan, Margush. 2013. "A Patient Is Healed by the Sound of a Drum." *Shamanism Annual* 26 (December):32-34.

King, Alexander. 2013. "Soul-Suckers: Dangerous Shamans among the Koryak People of Kamchatka." *Sacred Hoop* 82:14-20.

Kister, Daniel. 2004. "Korean Shamanism." Pp. 681-688 in Walter & Fridman.

Knecht, Peter. 2004. "Japanese Shamanism." Pp. 674-681 in Walter & Fridman.

Konstantinos. 2004. *Speak with the Dead: Seven Methods for Spirit Communication.* Woodbury, MN: Llewellyn.

Kowalewski, David. 1980. "Protest Uses of Symbolic Politics." *Social Science Quarterly* 61, 1 (June):95-113.

_____. 2000. *Deep Power.* Huntington, NY: Nova Science.

_____. 2003. "Vigilantism." Pp. 339-349 in Wilhelm Heitmeyer & John Hagan (eds.), *International Handbook of Research on Violence.* Heidelberg, Germany: Kluwer Academic.

_____. 2004. "Metaphysical Tracking: The Oldest Ecopsychology." *International Journal of Transpersonal Studies* 23:65-74.

_____. 2007. "Plant-Spirit Medicine: Mystical Phytopharmaceuticals in an Old (and New) Key." *Canadian Journal of Herbalism* 27, 3 (Summer):3-18.

_____. 2012. "Real or Imaginex? Truth and Fiction in Shamanic Journeys." *Journal of Shamanic Practice* 5, 2 (Fall):24-27.

_____. 2012a. "Organizational Soul-Thieves: A Shamanic Take on Bureaupathology." *Journal of Transpersonal Psychology* 44, 2:164-181.

_____. 2012b. "Shamanic Protocol—the Journey." *Sacred Hoop* 76:35-37.

_____. 2014. "The Call to Be a Shaman." *Sacred Hoop* 84 (2014):38-41.

Kowalewski, David, & Lara de la Iglesia. 2014. "Psychoppomps: Why They Matter." *Journal for Spiritual and Consciousness Studies* 37, 1 (January):5-13.

Kroeber, Theodora. 1961. *Ishi in Two Worlds*. Berkeley, CA: University of California Press.

Kübler-Ross, Elisabeth 1991. *On Life after Death*. Berkeley, CA: Celestial Arts.

Kyle, David. 1993. *Human Robots and Holy Mechanics*. Portland, OR: Swan/Raven.

LaGrand, Louis. 2006. *Love Lives On: Learning from the Expanding Encounters of the Bereaved*. New York, NY: Berkley.

Larramendi, Ana. 2010. "Healing the Spirit of Place." *Journal of Shamanic Practice* 3, 1 (April):29-34.

Laszlo, Ervin, & Anthony Peake. 2014. *Immortal Mind: Science and the Continuity of Consciousness beyond the Brain*. Rochester, VT: Inner Traditions.

Laughlin, Charles. 2004. "Navajo Shamanism." Pp. 318-323 in Walter & Fridman.

Lawrence, Lee. 2015. "A Feeling of Total and Complete Nirvana." *Searchlight: Newsletter of the Academy for Spiritual and Consciousness Studies* 24, 2 (April):7.

Leary, Mark. 2012. *Understanding the Mysteries of Human Behavior*. Chantilly, VA: Teaching Company.

Lee, R. 2010. "The New Pandemic: SuperStress?" *Explore: The Journal of Science and Healing* 6, 1:7-10.

Lepp, Trisha. 2004. "Psychopomp." Pp. 217-218 in Walter & Fridman.

Lester, David. 2005. *Is There Life after Death?* Jefferson, NC: McFarland.

Lewis, Todd. 2004. "Buddhism and Shamanism." Pp. 30-34 in Walter & Fridman.

Lewis-Williams, J., & T. Dowson. 1988. "Signs of All Times: Entopic Phenomena in Upper Paleolithic Art." *Current Anthropology* 29, 2 (April):201-217.

Linde, Andrei. 2004. "Inflation, Quantum Cosmology, and the Anthropic Principle." Pp. 440-460 in J. Barrow, P. Davies, & C. Harper (eds.), *Science and Ultimate Reality.* Cambridge, UK: Cambridge University Press.

Lindstrom, T.C. 1995. "Experiencing the Presence of the Dead." *Omega: An International Journal for the Study of Dying, Death, Bereavement, Suicide, and Other Lethal Behaviors* 31, 1:11-21.

Long, Jeffrey, & Paul Perry. 2010. *Evidence of the Afterlife: The Science of Near-Death Experiences.* New York, NY: HarperOne.

McCall, John. 2004. "Igbo Shamanism." Pp. 925-928 in Walter & Fridman.

Madden, Kristin. 1999. *Shamanic Guide to Death and Dying.* St. Paul, MN: Llewellyn.

Maher, Michaeleen, & George Hansen. 1995. "Quantitative Investigation of a 'Haunted Castle' in New Jersey." *Journal of the American Society for Psychical Research* 89 (January):19-50.

Malia, Linda. 2001. "A Fresh Look at a Remarkable Document." *Anglican Theological Review* 83, 1:65-88.

Marriot, Gordon. 2006. "Houses for a Spirit." *Sacred Hoop* 51:15.

Maxfield, Marilyn. 1994. "The Journey of the Drum." *ReVision* 16, 4 (Spring):157-163.

Moen, Bruce. 2014. "Retrieval: Being of Service Here and Then." Pp. 83-96 in Hogan.

Morse, M., & P. Perry. 1992. *Transformed by the Light: The Powerful Effects of Near-Death Experiences on People's Lives.* New York, NY: Villard.

Moss, Robert. 2006a. "Dreaming with the Departed." *Sacred Hoop* 51:12-14.

_____. 2006b. "Dream Visitations with the Dead." *Shaman's Drum* 72:12-18.

Murray, M., & J. Pizzorno. 1998. *Encyclopedia of Natural Medicine*. Rocklin, CA: Prima.

Myers, F.W.H. 2005. *Human Personality and Its Survival of Bodily Death*. Mineola, NY: Dover.

Neimark, Jill. 2003. "New Life for Near-Death." *Spirituality and Health* (September-October):43-45 & 73.

Noll, Richard. 1985. "Mental Imagery Cultivation as a Cultural Phenomenon: The Role of Visions in Shamanism." *Current Anthropology* 26, 4 (August-October):443-451.

_____. 2004. "Spirits and Souls." Pp. 235-238 in Walter & Fridman.

Noory, George, & Rosemary Guiley. 2011. *Talking to the Dead*. New York, NY: Tom Doherty Associates.

Omega Institute. 2002 & 2003. Gathering of the Shamans. Rhinebeck, NY.

Ornstein, Robert, & David Sobel. 1987. *Healing Brain: A Scientific Reader*. New York, NY: Guilford.

Oschman, James. 2000. *Energy Medicine: The Scientific Basis*. London, U.K.: Churchill Livingstone.

Osis, Karlis. 1979. "Scientific Evidence of Life after Death." *Journal of Religion and Psychical Research* 2, 3 (July):155-156.

Ostrander, Sheila, & Lynn Schroeder. 1997. *Psychic Discoveries*. Berkeley, CA: Marlowe.

Overton, James. 2000. "Neurocognitive Foundations of the Shamanic Perspective." *Shaman* 8, 1 (Spring):35-88.

Paasche, Klaus. 2013. "Healing the Lost Souls of Stalingrad." *Sacred Hoop* 82:31-36.

Palmer, G., & W. Braud. 2002. "Exceptional Human Experiences, Disclosure, and a More Inclusive View of Physical, Psychology, and Spiritual Well-Being." *Journal of Transpersonal Psychology* 34:29-61.

Peake, Anthony. 2009. *Is There Life after Death? Why Science Is Taking the Idea of an Afterlife Seriously.* London, UK: Arcturus.

Pennebaher, J. 1999. "The Effects of Traumatic Disclosure on Physical and Mental Health." *Mental Health* 1, 1:9-18.

Peters, Larry. 1981. "An Experiential Study of Nepalese Shamanism." *Journal of Transpersonal Psychology* 13, 1:1-26.

_____. 2010. "Shaman as Psychopomp: Field Report on the Foundation's Tibetan Living Treasures." *Shamanism Annual* 23 (December):25-29.

Pratt, Christina. 2007. *An Encyclopedia of Shamanism.* New York, NY: Rosen.

Radin, Dean. 1997. *Conscious Universe: The Scientific Truth of Psychic Phenomena.* New York, NY: Harper Edge.

_____. 2006. *Entangled Minds: Extrasensory Experiences in a Quantum Reality.* New York, NY: Paraview.

_____. 2013. *Supernormal: Science, Yoga, and the Evidence for Extraordinary Psychic Abilities.* New York, NY: Deepak Chopra Books.

_____, L. Michel, K. Goldamez, P. Wendland, R. Rickenbach, & A. Delorme. 2012. "Consciousness and the Double-Slit Interference Pattern." *Physics Essays* 25, 2:157-171, published online at physicsessays.org (16 May).

Rain, Mary Summer. 1989. *Phantoms Afoot.* Norfolk, VA: Donning.

Read, Donna. 1990. *Burning Times*. Santa Monica, CA: Direct Cinema Limited.

Reader's Digest. 2008. *Unseen World*. Pleasantville, NY.

Ring, Ken. 1989. "Near-Death and UFO Encounters as Shamanic Initiations: Some Conceptual and Evolutionary Implications." *ReVision* 11, 3 (Winter):14-22.

_____. 2006. *Lessons from the Light: What We Can Learn from the Near-Death Experience*. Needham, MA: Moment Point.

Roberts, G., & J. Owen. 1988. "The Near-Death Experience." *British Journal of Psychiatry* 153:607-617.

Robertson, Tricia. 2013. *Things You Can Do When You're Dead*. Guildford, U.K.: White Crow.

Robinson, Dana. 1998. Death and Dying. Workshop, Foundation for Shamanic Studies. Columbus, OH.

Rogers, Tom. 2009. "Our Last Stone Age Man." *Backwoodsman* 30, 6 (Autumn):62-66.

Rominger, R. 2009. "Exploring the Integration of Near-Death Experience Aftereffects: Summary of Findings." *Journal of Near-Death Studies* 28 (1), 3-34.

Rosenblatt, P., R.Walsh, & D. Johnson. 1976. *Grief and Mourning in Cross-Cultural Perspective*. N.p.: Human Relations Area Files.

Rummel, R.J. 1997. *Death by Government*. New York, NY: Transaction.

Rysdyk, Evelyn. 2015. "On the Wings of Garuda: A Group Psychopomp Ritual for Nepal." *Sacred Hoop* 88:32-33.

Sagan, Sam. 1997. *Entity Possession*. Rochester, VT: Destiny.

Sartori, Penny. 2014. *The Wisdom of Near-Death Experiences*. London, UK: Watkins.

Schmeidler, Gertrude. 1966. "Quantitative Investigation of a 'Haunted House.'" *Journal of the American Society for Psychical Research* 60:137-149.

Schnabel, Jim. 1997. *Remote-Viewers: The Secret History of America's Psychic Spying.* New York, NY: Dell.

Schwalm, Maurice. 1995. "Haunted Mountain." *Journal of Religion and Psychical Research* 18, 3 (July):165.

Selye, H. 1978. *Stress of Life.* New York, NY: McGraw-Hill.

Sheldrake, Rupert. 2011. *Dogs That Know When Their Owners Are Coming Home.* Portland, OR: Broadway.

_____, & Michael Lambert. 2007. "An Automated Online Telepathy Test." *Journal of Scientific Exploration* 21, 3:511-522.

Sifers, Sarah. 2003. "Fate of the Pau: Three Tibetan Shamans' Stories." *Shamanism* 16 (2):15-29.

Silvana, Laura Aversano. 2009. *Plant Spirit Journey.* Woodbury, MN: Llewellyn.

Sluten, Mary. 2015. "Spiritual Appropriation in Contemporary Shamanic Practice." *Sacred Hoop* 88:44-48.

Smith, Jeremy. 2015. *Epic Measures: One Doctor, Seven Billion Patients.* New York, NY: HarperWave.

Solomon, George. 1990. "The Energy Field of Psychoneuroimmunology, with a Special Note on AIDS." Pp. 182-203 in Robert Ornstein & Charles Swencionis (eds), *Healing Brain: A Scientific Reader.* New York, NY: Guilford.

Sounds True. 2008. *Measuring the Immeasureable: The Scientific Case for Spirituality.* Boulder, CO.

Starfield, B. 2000. "Is U.S. Health Really the Best in the World?" *Journal of the American Medical Association* 284, 4 (July 26):483-485.

Steinhart, Peter. 1995. *The Company of Wolves*. New York, NY: Vintage.

Stevenson, Ian. 1992. "A Series of Possibly Paranormal Recurrent Dreams." *Journal of Scientific Exploration* 6, 3:281-289.

_____. 1995. "Six Modern Apparitional Experiences." *Journal of Scientific Exploration* 9, 3:351-366.

Stout, Jolaine, Linda Jacquin, & P.M.H. Atwater. 2006. "Six Major Challenges Faced by Near-Death Experiencers." *Journal of Near-Death Studies* 25, 1 (Fall):49-62.

Sullivan, T.A. 2012. *Escorting the Dead: My Live as a Psychopomp*. New York, NY: CreateSpace.

_____, & N. Sullivan. 2013. *Soul Rescuers Manual*. Hammersmith, UK: Thorsons.

Sutherland, Cherie. 1989. "Psychic Phenomena Following Near-Death Experiences." *Journal of Near-Death Studies* 8, 2 (Winter):93-102.

Targ, Russell, & Harold Puthoff. 1977. *Mind Reach: Scientists Look at Psychic Ability*. New York, NY: Delacorte.

Tart, Charles. 2004. "On the Scientific Foundations of Transpersonal Psychology." *Journal of Transpersonal Psychology* 36, 1:66-90.

_____. 2009. *End of Materialism: How Evidence of the Paranormal Is Bringing Science and Spirit Together*. Oakland, CA: New Harbinger.

Taylor, Greg. 2009. "Death before Life after Life." *Darklore* 3:47-67.

_____. 2014. "Dying Light." *Darklore* 8:243-250.

Tein, Tassan, D. Shumkin, & S. Kan. 1994. "Shamans of the Siberian Eskimos." *Arctic Anthropology* 31, 1:117-127.

Tick, Edward. 2007. "Healing Mysteries in a Vietnamese Village." *Explore* 3, 2 (March-April):150-161.

_____. 2013. "Wandering Souls of Vietnam." *Journal of Contemporary Shamanism* 6, 1 (Spring):17-19.

Tunney, Carol. 2013. "Shamanism in the Surgical Suite." Pp. 85-106 in Carson.

Turk, Jon. 2009. *Raven's Gift: A Scientist, A Shaman, and Their Remarkable Journey through the Siberian Wilderness.* New York, NY: St. Martin's Griffin.

Turner, Edith. 1992. "The Reality of Spirits." *ReVision* 15, 1:28-32.

Turner, Kevin. 2013. "When Shamans Climb Trees II." *Shamanism Annual* 26 (December):2-9.

Tymn, Michael. 2002. "Mediumship: Direct Connection to a Level of the Afterlife, Telepathy, or Fraud?" *Journal of Religion and Psychical Research* 25, 3 (July):123-134.

Utts, Jessica. 1996. "An Assessment of the Evidence for Psychic Functioning." *Journal of Scientific Exploration* 10, 1:3-30.

Vallee, Jacques. 1994. "Anatomy of a Hoax." *Journal of Scientific Exploration* 8, 1:47-71.

van Lommel, Pim. 2011. *Consciousness beyond Life.* New York, NY: HarperOne.

Varga, Jose. 2009. *Visits from Heaven.* Virginia Beach, VA: ARE Press.

Villoldo, Alberto. 1998. Incan Shamanism. Workshop, Omega Institute, Rhinebeck, NY.

Vuckovic, N., C. Gullion, M. Ramirez, J. Schneider, & L. Williams. 2007. "Feasibility and Short-Term Outcomes of a Shamanic Treatment for Temporomandibular Joint Disorders." *Alternative Therapies in Health and Medicine* 13, 6 (November-December):18-29.

Vyse, S. 1997. *Believing in Magic*. New York, NY: Oxford University Press.

Walker, Thomas. 2009. *The Force Is with Us: The Higher Consciousness that Science Refuses to Accept*. Wheaton, IL: Theosophical Publishing.

Walter, M. & E. Fridman (eds.). 2004. *Shamanism: An Encyclopedia of World Beliefs, Practices, and Culture*. Oxford, U.K.: ABC-CLIO.

Wangyal, Tenzin. 2004. Tibetan Bön Shamanism. Workshop, Omega Institute, Rhinebeck, NY.

Walsh, Roger. 1989. "The Shamanic Journey: Experiences, Origins, and Analogues." *ReVision* 12, 2 (Fall):25-32.
___. 2007. *World of Shamanism*. Woodbury, MN: Llewellyn.

White, J. 2012. *Practical Guide to Death and Dying*. New York, NY: Cosimo.

Wicker, Christine. 2009. "How Spiritual Are We?" *Parade* (4 October):4-5.

Wickham, Alasdair. 2011. *The Dead Roam the Earth*. New York, NY: Penguin.

Wilson, Colin. 2008. *Beyond the Occult: Twenty Years' Research into the Paranormal*. London, U.K.: Watkins.
_____. 2011. *Supernatural*. London, U.K.: Watkins.

Wilcox, Joan. 2004. *Masters of the Living Energy: The Mystical World of the Q'ero of Peru*. Rochester, VT: Inner Traditions.

Winkowski, Mary Ann. 2009. *When Ghosts Speak*. New York, NY: Grand Central.

Wood, Nicholas Breeze. 2015. "Phowa: A Simple Practice of Healing and Compassion for the Dying and the Newly Dead." *Sacred Hoop* 88:40-41.

Wooley, Dan. 2010. *Unshaken: Rising from the Ruins of Haiti's Hotel Montana*. Peabody, MA: Zondervan.

Wright, Sylvia Hart. 1998. "Experiences of Spontaneous Psychokinesis after Bereavement." *Journal of the Society for Psychical Research* 62, 852 (July):385-395.

_____. 2004. "What Happens after Death?" *Journal of Religion and Psychical Research* 27, 1 (January):7-9.

_____. 2008. "Over a Century of Research on After-Death Communication." *Journal of Spirituality and Paranormal Studies* 31, 3 (July):154-166.

About the Author

Twice a Fulbright scholar and twice a U.S. National Endowment for the Humanities grantee, David Kowalewski, PhD, has been practicing shamanism for several decades. His research on shamanism, religion, and the paranormal has appeared in *Journal of Contemporary Shamanism*, *Journal of Shamanic Practice*, *Journal of Transpersonal Psychology*, *Journal for the Scientific Study of Religion*, *Review of Religious Research*, *Journal of Church and State*, *Sociology of Religion*, and *International Journal of Transpersonal Studies*. He has studied with the shamans of many continents, and is a graduate of extended training by the Foundation for Shamanic Studies, including its Three-Year Program in Advanced Shamanic Initiation.

Printed in the United States
By Bookmasters